ENGLAND
RUGBY

THE

# ENGLAND
# RUGBY

## SCRAPBOOK

ENGLAND
RUGBY

THE

# ENGLAND
# RUGBY

Sport Media
A Trinity Mirror Business

Published by Trinity Mirror Sport Media
Managing Director: Ken Rogers
Senior Editor: Steve Hanrahan
Editor: Paul Dove
Senior Art Editor: Rick Cooke

Writers: Chris Brereton, Alan Jewell
Production: Adam Oldfield
Design: Colin Sumpter, Alison Barkley

With special thanks to Jane Barron, Michael Rowe,
Patricia Mowbray and Deborah Mason at the RFU

First Edition
Published in hardback in Great Britain in 2013.
Published and produced by: Trinity Mirror Sport Media,
PO Box 48, Old Hall Street, Liverpool L69 3EB.

ISBN: 9781908695529

Photography: World Rugby Musuem, RFU via Getty Images, Leo Wilkinson, Tony Woolliscroft, PA Images, Liverpool Daily Post & Echo, Mirrorpix

Printed and bound in Slovenia by arrangement with KINT Ljubljana

RFU Official Licensed Product

# So proud to have worn the Red Rose

**H**i, my name is Lawrence Dallaglio and welcome to The Official England Rugby Scrapbook. I played 85 times for England and that record fills me with a huge amount of pride. Even in my wildest dreams I never imagined I would get the chance to represent my country for so long or so often.

People always ask me who the best players were I played with and against and I'm very proud to say they were English or the majority of them were English. Those guys were the very best in the world.

I grew up very close to Twickenham so I've seen the whole stadium evolve over a number of years.

I've seen the stadium go from 40,000 to its current 82,000 capacity and I've got some amazing memories of a ground that is rightly regarded as one of the best in the world.

I visited the ground as a spectator on a number of occasions. As a young lad I played here, using the width of the field for my primary school, and after scoring a try I remember thinking it was a long way to run!

I also came here to watch both domestic games and England matches when I was growing up. I watched the opening match of the 1991 World Cup and I was here on the day England lost the final to Australia. Thankfully, I've had some far better memories since then!

The word Twickenham has always been synonymous with English rugby and without sounding too arrogant about it, the game was developed and founded in England; this is where all the history and heritage is so it's wonderful to have played here.

I felt, and still feel, it is a very special place.

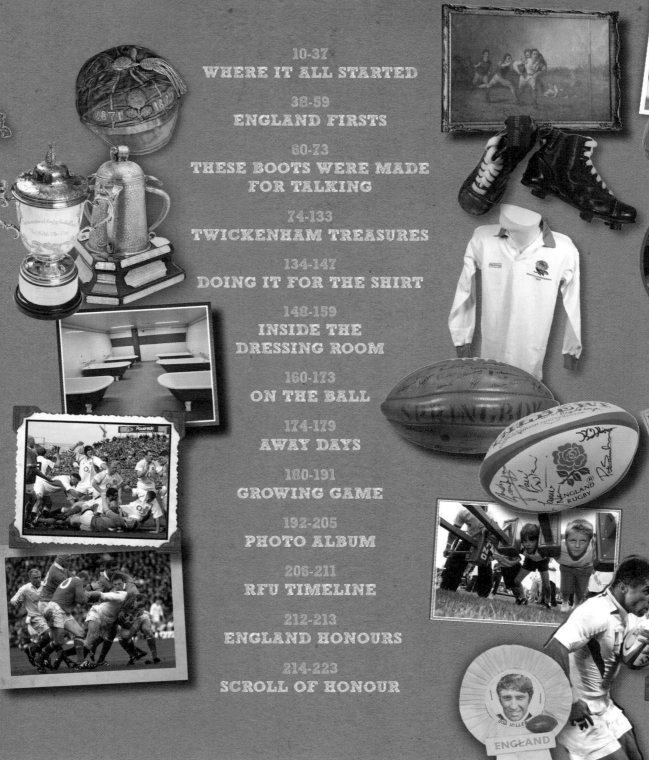

# CONTENTS

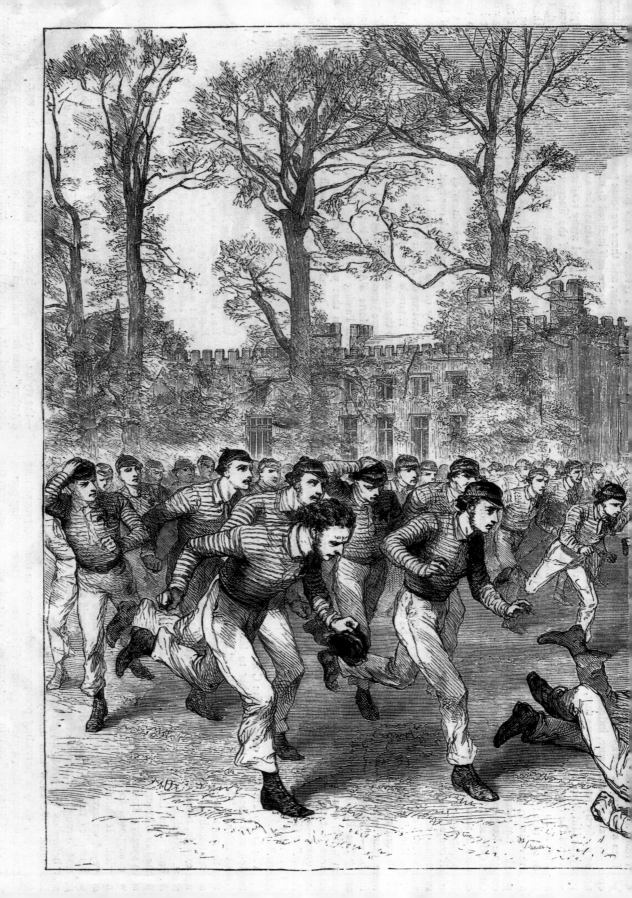

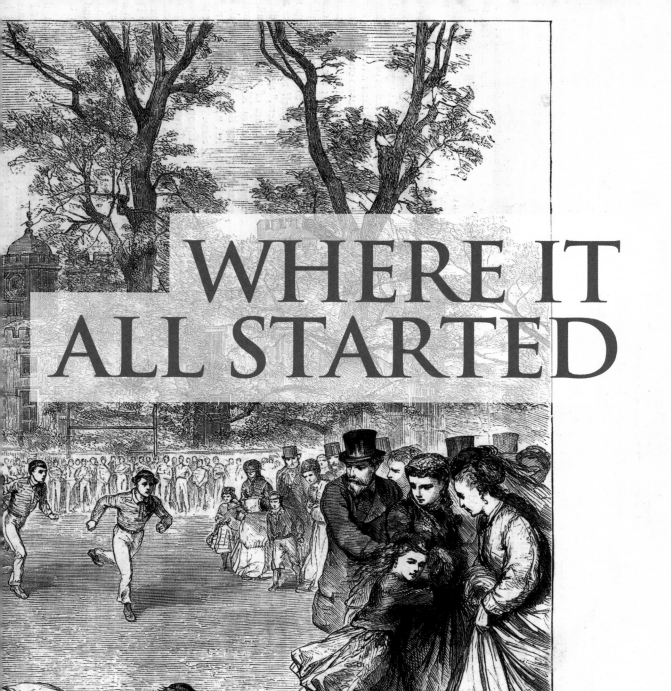

# WHERE IT ALL STARTED

**A charge for possession during this 1870 depiction of a game in progress at Rugby School**

W.Thomas.S?

# The birth of rugby

Everyone knows rugby's origins don't they? William Webb Ellis picked up the ball while playing football at Rugby School in 1823 and the sport was born.

Well, not exactly.

Rugby School started the process of codifying the game that we recognise today but, in fact, many different forms of football had existed for a long time before Webb Ellis came into the picture.

And even then, some consider the idea that the Rugby pupil inspired the sport a myth, created long after Webb Ellis had left the school.

The real origins of rugby lie in the raucous free-for-all matches that sometimes involved the menfolk of whole towns and villages. These encounters, littered across Britain, were brutal affairs with no formal kit, no hard rules and no real time limit.

The aim of those early games was to get the ball to a certain marker in the opposition's territory – it could be a pub wall, a tree or the village hall – by any means necessary.

Lips would get split and bones would get broken and, as is often the case when local pride is at stake, games were interrupted by mass brawling.

The earliest record of a game taking place dates back to 828AD but the violent nature of the game did not please everybody and was even banned by King Edward II in 1314 for being too rowdy – a royal decree that would stay in place in various different forms until well into the 17th century.

As the centuries passed, public schools began devising their own version of 'football' and Rugby School was no different.

With games played on the pitch at 'School Close' – a patch of ground

**The Rugby School house caps, *above*, and, *right*, the coat of arms**

containing no less than three elm trees – pupils at Rugby would roll their sleeves up and play in matches involving hundreds of players, but no referee.

Although each match could see a completely new set of rules – decided beforehand by the respective captains – points were generally scored by kicking between the uprights. For the scorer to be given the opportunity to 'try' to kick the ball through the posts, they must first touch the ball down over the oppositions goal-line.

That is where the idea of a 'try' comes from and why its title remains that to this day.

Well before Webb Ellis supposedly made his mark, catching and throwing the ball was

**Boys in their Rugby School kit in 1846**

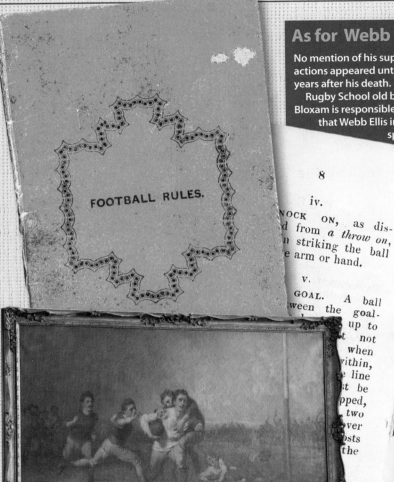

### 8

**iv.**
NOCK ON, as dis-
d from *a throw on*,
striking the ball
e arm or hand.

**v.**
GOAL. A ball
ween the goal-
up to
t not
when
ithin,
e line
t be
pped,
two
ver
sts
the

### 9

dress or person of any player.
No goal may be kicked from touch.

**vi.**
KICK OFF FROM MIDDLE, must be a place.

**vii.**
KICK OUT must not be from more than ten yards out of goal if a place-kick, not more than twenty-five yards, if a punt, drop, or knock on.

**viii.**
RUNNING IN is allowed to any player on his side, provided he does not take the ball off the ground, or take it through touch.

allowed, although it wasn't until the 1830s that a pupil called Jem Mackie popularised the idea of running with the ball and 'running in' a try.

Eventually it was decided that the sport needed a more formal set of rules so in August 1845, three of the school's pupils – William Delafield Arnold, W.W. Shirley and Frederick Hutchins – sat down and devised the sport's first formal regulations.

The document was by no means a complete set of instructions, as the game's shape and style continued to change over the coming decades.

But the fact Rugby School had written down their rules first helped set their version of the sport on the path to world domination.

**The first laws of the sport, *top*, published in 1845; *left*: a painting showing an early encounter; *right*: a sketch of the playing fields at Rugby School in 1817**

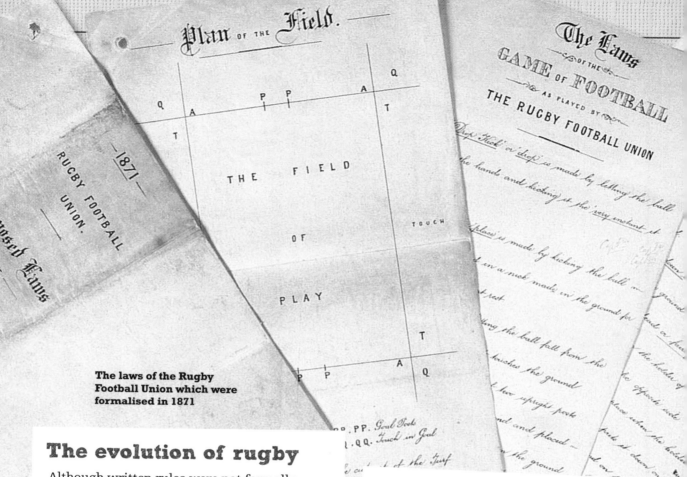

The laws of the Rugby Football Union which were formalised in 1871

# The evolution of rugby

Although written rules were not formally devised until 1845, the Rugby School version had grown into one of the most popular forms of the sport by that time as former students took the game with them once they went on to university and beyond.

At Cambridge University in 1839, Old Rugbeian Arthur Pell formed a football team and although he did not know it at the time, he had begun the slow march towards the foundation of the Football Association and the later creation of the Rugby Football Union.

Pell's side, made up mainly of fellow Old Rugbeians, took on a team of Old Etonians, but disagreements followed as the Old Rugbeians insisted on catching the ball and using their hands – just as they had been taught at school.

However, at Eton, handling the ball had been outlawed and the difference in the two sides' interpretations of the rules prompted the idea that a more general set of laws were required so that teams from different parts of the country could play each other.

That led to the 'Cambridge Rules' of 1848 which formalised the use of goal-kicks, throw-ins, off-sides and other laws that are still recognisable in the game of football today.

Eventually, the desire to tighten up the Cambridge Rules grew even further, so 12 leading football clubs met in the Freemasons' Tavern in Great Queen Street in London in 1863 and tried to find enough common ground to formulate one set of laws.

All was going to plan until the fifth meeting when it was proposed that running with the ball and 'hacking' (kicking opponents in the shin) should be outlawed.

That was too much for Francis Maule Campbell, one of Blackheath Football Club's representatives at the meeting, and he withdrew his club from the discussions because he believed hacking demonstrated skill and courage. Other clubs followed his example and the split between association football and rugby had begun.

## The first president

While association football grew tremendously over the next decade, rugby also remained popular and found a huge new following in the north of England.

Eventually it was decided that – in a similar manner to the meetings of 1863 – one single set of laws needed to be set so teams from different areas could compete against each other.

On January 26, 1871, such a meeting was held at the Pall Mall restaurant on Regent Street.

Twenty-one clubs attended and the Rugby Football Union was born, with Algernon Rutter elected as the first president. Incidentally, 22 clubs should have been present but the representative from London Wasps missed the meeting and the rumour remains to this day that their man got lost on the way to Regent Street and then got too drunk to find the venue.

By June 1871, the necessary rules to codify the game had been completed and the game of rugby was finally formalised.

England match tickets from 1888 v Wales, and 1903 v Scotland; *below:* the first president of the RFU, Algernon Rutter

## Breaking with tradition

One of the central and proudest tenets of rugby was the idea that the game was amateur. The sport's rulers felt it was within the Corinthian tradition that had been instilled in them at public school that men should wish to play simply for the honour and physical exercise.

However, this view was at odds with many clubs, particularly those in the north of England. While those in the south may have been able to play the game for nothing, many players in the north had to take time off work if they wanted to represent their town or club.

As a result of this, many clubs wanted to introduce 'broken-time' payments to players, meaning they would not be left out of pocket if they missed a morning's work to play rugby.

This practice became increasingly widespread in the 1880s and 1890s before a vote to try and legalise 'broken-time' payments was easily defeated in an RFU vote in September 1893.

The RFU's decision angered many northern clubs and eventually led to the famous meeting at the George Hotel, Huddersfield, on August 29, 1895.

Over 20 clubs from Cheshire, Yorkshire and Lancashire decided to break away from the RFU and they created the Northern Rugby Football Union (NRFU).

The NRFU, which eventually changed its name to the Rugby Football League in 1923, allowed players to be paid in order to safeguard the livelihoods of the working men who played it.

However, rugby union stuck determinedly to its amateur status until 1995 when it finally turned professional – a move that was needed if the game was going to continue to prosper in an ever more lucrative sporting world.

*Rugby Football Union*

First
General Meeting, held at the
Pall Mall Restaurant - Charing Cross - London -
January - 26th 1871

Mr E. C. Holmes in the Chair.

Present - F. Stokes and B. H. Burns (Blackheath), E. Rutter (Richmond), W. F. Eaton (Ravenscourt Park), F. I. Currey (Marlborough Nomads), A. G. Guillemard (West Kent), L. J. Maton (Wimbledon Hornets), F. Luscombe & I. W. Smith (Gipsies), C. Herbert & H. Wood (Civil Service), R. Leigh (Law Club), A. J. English (Wellington College), J. H. Ewart (Guy's Hospital), F. Hartley (Flamingoes), W. E. Rowlinson (Clapham Rovers), C. E. Atkinson (Harlequins), E. M. Madden & C. E. Pope (King's College), W. Hooper & G. E. Gregory (St Paul's School), E. C. Hill (Queen's House), F. Noone & I. Devonport (Lausanne), H. Graham (Addison), R. J. Buckland & G. Ellis (Mohicans)

**Notes from the first general meeting of the RFU**

FAIRFIELD ESTATE.
TWICKENHAM.

THE RUGBY UNION
TWICKENHAM GROUND

BLOCK PLAN

**The changing face of Twickenham is shown in these early plans**

**England take on New Zealand at Twickenham in 1925, the ground now firmly established as the home of English rugby**

# The birth of Twickenham

Twickenham may well be synonymous with English rugby but the national side existed long before 'The Cabbage Patch' became England's famous and permanent home.

Before the stadium's first game – played between Harlequins and Richmond on October 2, 1909 – England had already played in places as far and wide as Leeds, Birkenhead and Leicester.

Originally, it was felt that England did not need a specific ground, but as the sport's popularity grew, so did the clamour to give the national side some firm foundations.

Money also played its part in convincing the RFU that a permanent home was required.

By the early 1900s, England were attracting impressive crowds – but the coffers remained empty.

Around 45,000 fans turned up to watch England v New Zealand at Crystal Palace in December 1905 and a further 40,000 the year after when England played South Africa.

Gate receipts were impressive – yet costs were high as the RFU had to rent temporary stadiums for the matches rather than pocket all the profit from the internationals.

As a result of this shortfall, influential RFU member William Cail proposed, on December 7 1906, that the RFU Finance Committee should seriously "consider the advisability or practicability of this Union purchasing a ground in or near London."

The RFU rubber-stamped the idea that England needed a permanent base. But where?

This is where William Williams intervened.

He was appointed by Cail to find the perfect location – and was given £7,500 in order to snap up what piece of land he felt was best suited to the RFU's aims.

Williams searched far and wide for the best location and after turning down spots in Blackheath and Richmond, in 1907 he made his mind up that Twickenham would be the perfect place to build a new stadium.

His decision did not impress everybody.

One critic called Twickenham "fearsomely remote from Piccadilly Circus" and the 10-and-a-quarter acre patch of land bought by Williams – for the princely sum of £5,572 12s and 6d – was deemed to be too much for what was little more than farmland.

However, history proves that Williams knew what he was doing – and the fact the land he purchased was used for farming also gave Twickenham its first nickname – 'The Cabbage Patch'.

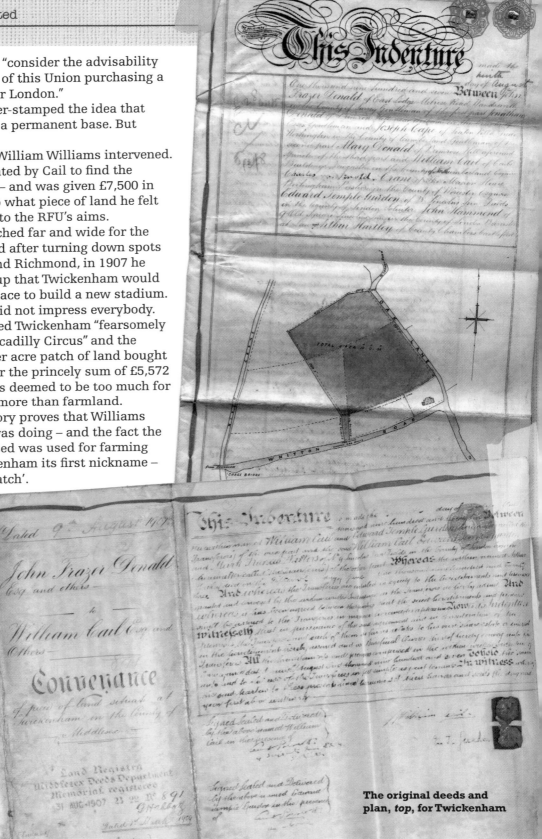

**The original deeds and plan, *top*, for Twickenham**

William Cail, *far right*, who put forward the idea that the RFU should purchase their own ground; while William Williams, *right*, was responsible for finding a suitable location, and decided upon Twickenham in 1907.

January 15, 1909     THE DAILY MIRROR.

RUGBY FOOTBALL SENSATION: SCOTLAND REFUSES TO MEET ENGLAND.

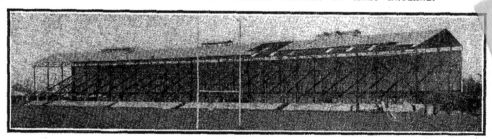

Consternation has been caused in Rugby football circles by the announcement that Scotland will not play England at Rugby this year. The crime of which England is accused is of having invited the Australians to this country knowing that the players would individually receive a guinea a week for incidental out-of-pocket expenses. The picture shows a stand on the Rugby Union's new ground at Twickenham.—(*Daily Mirror* photograph.)

As a result of the action of the Scottish Union, the time-honoured match for the Calcutta Cup, which is now held by Scotland, will not take place this season. (1) Building a stand on the Rugby Union's new ground at Twickenham. (2) Mr. C. J. B. Marriott, secretary of the English Rugby Union.
—(*Daily Mirror* photographs.)

## Payment row delays 1909 Calcutta Cup

Scotland originally refused to meet England in the spring of 1909 for the annual Calcutta Cup battle because of a row over player payments.

When England faced Australia in January, the visitors had been given a guinea a week in "out-of-pocket" expenses. Scotland originally opposed this decision but on March 20 the match did finally go ahead at Richmond, with Scotland winning 18-8.

THE DAILY MIRROR

# ENGLAND SCORES A BRILLIANT RUGBY VICTORY OVER WALES.

There were scenes of tremendous enthusiasm at Twickenham on Saturday, when England beat Wales in the Rugby international by a goal and a try (eight points) to nothing. (1) A breakaway by England. (2) An Englishman tackled. (3) An improvised grandstand outside the ground, showing jubilant Englishmen. (4) England's first try converted by F. E. Chapman. (5) England use their feet. (6) Crowd cheering England's goal.—(*Daily Mirror* and Sport and General.)

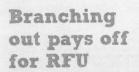

# Branching out pays off for RFU

Bumper crowds have always been part of the England experience.

Around 20,000 crammed into Twickenham in January 1912 to watch England beat Wales 8-0 in the Five Nations.

The option to build a rugby-specific stadium had been a gamble when the RFU decided to buy Twickenham in 1907, but their vision was instantly rewarded as fans flocked to west London from all over the country.

"IT'S THE HOME OF RUGBY. THERE'S SO MUCH HISTORY HERE AND TO HAVE A PACKED HOUSE CHEERING FOR YOU – IT JUST DOESN'T GET ANY BETTER. IT'S AN INCREDIBLY SPECIAL ARENA AND IT'S IMPORTANT THAT WE, AS ENGLISHMEN, MAKE THE MOST OF THE OPPORTUNITY."

## MY ENGLAND
### ALEX GOODE

## MY ENGLAND
### JOSH LEWSEY

"As a player, I didn't really give myself the indulgence of savouring the atmosphere or really breathing it in. You are so determined to perform at your best and deliver, for your country or your club, that the atmosphere at the time is something I could never really focus on. It is only later on and after your career that you look back on that time and that atmosphere and enjoy it. The time for nostalgia is afterwards. The are rare moments and occasions when you are playing and you do go 'wow' but you get more of those through hindsight than you do at the time. But the luxury of enjoying it is for afters – we had a job to do!

As a player, you want to deliver on the biggest stage, so you want to be professional, but you also remember that there is so much heritage at Twickenham; it is the home of English game."

# MY ENGLAND
## LEWIS MOODY

"Your emotions before the game are always the same; you hate it because you're so nervous and so desperate to win and impress and get things right. It is incredibly daunting when you're waiting to go out onto the pitch because you can hear all the noise. When you stand there waiting, it feels like you're about to head into The Coliseum! The noise starts to escalate through the big double green doors in front of you and when you get onto the pitch, there are fireworks, brass bands and the military right in front of you; you're lucky not to run into one of the flag-bearers or military men!

I remember I didn't distinguish anyone in the crowd when I was on the pitch, it was just like a wall of colour and noise that envelops you. It is a cacophony of noise and it feels like it blankets the stadium and it was a very surreal occasion."

"PLAYING AT TWICKENHAM IS A DREAM COME TRUE. I REALLY LOVE IT. GROWING UP I WOULDN'T HAVE CONSIDERED THAT I'D HAVE THE OPPORTUNITY TO PLAY FOR ENGLAND, SO TO END UP HERE AND TO BE PART OF THIS TEAM, WELL, IT'S THE BIGGEST HONOUR AND A HUGE PRIVILEGE."

# MY ENGLAND
## MANU TUILAGI

## MY ENGLAND
### JEFF PROBYN

"It's the home of English rugby and, as a young player, your ambitions are twofold. Firstly, you want to play representative rugby at any level and then you want to play for England. Most people only dream of that because you never really believe you'll get the chance to, but it's amazing when it happens. Running out to a full Twickenham is an intense experience.

In some ways you're too focused on the game to appreciate it. It's only in the years afterwards that you really appreciate how special it was. At the old Twickenham you were much, much closer to the crowd. When Brian Moore took a line-out he could literally shake hands with people in the crowd and that helped build up a very special relationship with spectators.

I scored a try against Ireland at home in 1990 and it was a great moment. It was one of my three tries for England.

Before coming out onto the pitch, you could hear the crowd in the West Car Park more than you could the crowd in the stadium; that's until you walked out through the tunnel and then you were hit with a wall of noise. In those days you practically walked through the crowd to get onto the pitch."

## MY ENGLAND
### BRAD BARRITT

"WHEN THE CROWD IS BEHIND YOU AT TWICKENHAM, IT CAN FEEL LIKE YOU'VE GOT 16 MEN ON THE PITCH. THE PLAYERS LOVE THAT."

# MY ENGLAND
### BEN KAY

"Twickenham is immense and everybody always warns you when you play your first international at Twickenham that it will just flash by and you will wonder where it went and where the game's gone and that is totally what happened. We beat the Australians as well which helps! I'd played at Twickenham before for Leicester, but to walk out for your country against the then world champions was very special.

I can remember walking out of the tunnel. It was a huge moment and the noise is incredible. It gives you a huge lift and when you stop playing for England, that is one thing you miss the most.

During a game you become attuned to the noise levels, but then when England attacked and the crowd level rose again, it reminded you of just how loud the crowd can be. The volume ramps up to another level, and that's when you remember Twickenham is a special place."

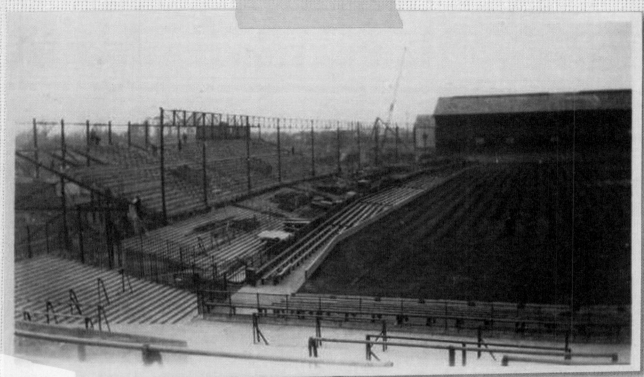

Early construction work at Twickenham increased the stadium's capacity to 20,000. It included redevelopment of the Northern Terrace, the East Stand and the South Terrace, while a new West Stand, complete with offices, was built in 1932.

1931

1932

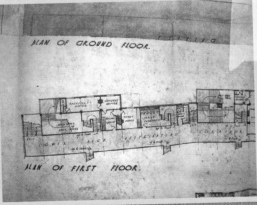

PLAN OF GROUND FLOOR.

PLAN OF FIRST FLOOR.

Twickenham undergoes one it's biggest, and most controversial, renovations during the late '70s and early '80s, but after initial resistance from local residents, the new-look South Stand was opened in 1981.

1978-1981

# The changing face of Twickenham

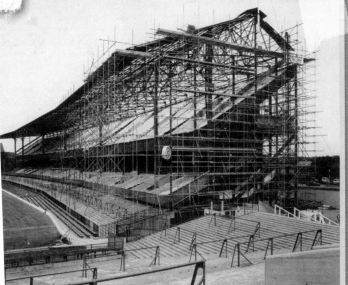

Twickenham has gone through a series of developments to get to the ultra-modern, all-seater facility we have today.

The first major renovation occurred between the wars. In 1921, a stand was built above the Northern Terrace, while the East Stand and South Terrace were extended later in the decade. In 1932, a West Stand was built, featuring offices for the RFU.

Structural failings caused the closure of the South Terrace in 1965. It was decided that it would be cheaper to build a new stand but, due to objections from local residents, planning permission was not granted until 1978, with the new South Stand finally opening in 1981.

The most dramatic changes have occurred over the past 25 years. The North Stand

»

1981

was taken down in 1988, reopening as a three-tier structure in 1990. The new look was extended to include the West Stand after the 1992 Five Nations, with the development complete the following year. In 1995, the West Stand followed suit, increasing the capacity to 75,000.

In 2002, the decision was taken to rebuild the South Stand, with work commencing in 2005. As well as increasing the capacity to 82,000 (the largest rugby stadium in the world), the development included a four-star hotel, a performing arts complex, a health and leisure club and a new rugby shop.

The South Stand was complete for the 2006 autumn international series, but the modernising work continues ahead of the 2015 Rugby World Cup. The North and West Stands are to be modernised, with a slight increase in capacity expected, and the upgrading of corporate hospitality facilities.

A new pitch was installed in the summer of 2012, with three per cent artificial grass to stabilise the surface.

Mid-tier LED screens, which relate messages to supporters, are already operational, while new TV screens for all the concourses and high-density wi-fi will also be in place well before the Rugby World Cup arrives.

1970

1991

1999

2001

Groundstaff clear
a snow-covered
Twickenham pitch
as the new 14,800-
seat North Stand
is completed, *top*,
while a new West
Stand was next to
be developed in
1995.

WELCOME TO
TWICKENHAM
THE HOME OF ENGLAND RUGBY

## A picnic in the (car) park

Twickenham may have changed size and shape on many occasions but one aspect remains constant; the pre-match picnic in the West Car Park.

As these pictures show, ranging from the 1960s Varsity Match to the 2013 Six Nations, thousands of supporters, from all sides and all nationalities, meet up in the West Car Park to eat, drink, catch up with old friends, tease old foes and prepare for that afternoon's entertainment.

A view of Twickenham, dated 2007. The stadium has undergone many changes over the years but is now regarded as the number one rugby venue in the world

# Stadium fit for world's best

An overview of Twickenham, the ultra-modern stadium which is to become the focal point of the 2015 Rugby World Cup. Additional upgrades are scheduled ahead of the six-week showpiece, further adding to its reputation as the number one rugby destination. From these images, it's hard to believe the venue was once a humble cabbage patch.

THE RUGBY STORE
TWICKENHAM

MUSEUM OF RUGBY
TWICKENHAM

ENGLAND RUGBY WALL OF SUPPORT

EAS

THE SPIRIT OF RUGBY

## Taking international rugby back to its grass roots

A lot of work goes on behind the scenes to ensure Twickenham is fit for match days. Groundstaff use modern, scientific techniques to manage and maintain the manicured lawn, delivering a playing surface to be proud of.

## Greatest show on turf

From a 'Cabbage Patch' to one of the best pitches in the world – welcome to the Twickenham turf; a clean, green space-age machine.

Until 2012, players gracing the Twickenham pitch were playing on a surface that had barely changed in over a century of rugby battle.

However, the looming 2015 Rugby World Cup inspired the RFU to redesign the pitch and give Twickenham a playing surface that has made it the envy of the sporting world.

And the numbers involved are almost as staggering as the end product.

Over 9,000 tonnes of old pitch were removed, 20 miles of undersoil heating pipes were laid, new irrigation and drainage were installed, six tonnes of nutrients were added and 300kg of hardy rye grass seed was planted.

And here is the really amazing part.

As well as natural grass, 20 million strands of artificial grass were also sewn into the pitch, adding extra stability. If those strands were laid end-to-end, they would stretch out for 30,000 miles and easily encircle the planet.

Head Groundsman Keith Kent said: "We are confident that this pitch is the very, very top of the range and we are delighted with it.

"I'm so proud of all my staff and also the RFU for being willing to invest in a pitch that should last us for a long time.

"When the World Cup arrives, we are confident the pitch will look as good at the end of the tournament as it will at the start.

"My job is unique; one week I can be marking out a pitch for a Six Nations match and the next pitch I mark out could be for a school competition.

"The pitch is used by so many different levels of the game and that gives us all a thrill. It is not just here for international players – it is here for everyone."

# The spirit of Twickenham

Few stadiums in world rugby resonate and roar as much as Twickenham when the opening chorus lines of 'Swing Low Sweet Chariot' are heartily sung by a full house on match days.

But how did an African-American spiritual song, written in Oklahoma in the mid-19th century, become the trademark sound of English rugby?

The answer goes back to March 18, 1988 and to a time when the national side was struggling to entertain. In fact, the Twickenham crowd had only seen a solitary England try in the previous two years.

At half-time during a Five Nations fixture against Ireland, England were 3-0 down, courtesy of a Michael Kiernan drop-goal in the last minute of the first half.

Exciting it was not.

In fact, the pre-match words of England coach Geoff Cooke looked set to come back and haunt him. He had told the assembled press that his players believed that "one day they are going to go out and stuff someone."

But on that afternoon in west London, nobody would have believed today was that day.

Yet, in the second period, the form book and England's style of play were turned on their heads.

Scrum-half and captain Nigel Melville had broken his leg seconds before the end of the first half and that meant replacement No.9 Richard Harding had to step in.

He immediately brought more pace and direction to England's attacking play and before anybody knew it, England were scoring tries for fun, running rampant in an eventual 35-3 victory.

Three of those tries came in super-quick succession from Chris Oti – England's Nigerian-born winger making his Twickenham debut.

In fact, before anyone knew it, Oti had scored Twickenham's first hat-trick for 64 years – and all in under 11 minutes.

In tribute to their new hero, a group of students in the Lower East Stand launched into a rendition of 'Swing Low' – a song that had long been a bar, dressing room and common room favourite across the country.

With every score Oti managed, the volume and number of singers increased until the entire stadium was a cacophony of noise.

And it has been that way ever since.

SINGING THE NATIONAL ANTHEM

"FOR ME, THE MOST IMPORTANT THING IS KNOWING THAT THE PEOPLE YOU LOVE ARE PROUD OF WHAT YOU DO AND WHAT YOU ARE ACHIEVING. YOU'RE SINGING THE NATIONAL ANTHEM, YOU LOOK UP TO THE SKY, AND THERE'S NO BETTER FEELING."

MY ENGLAND
MANU TUILAGI

MY ENGLAND
RICHARD HILL

"I had been warned that the stadium noise might get to me. I began to realise what I was heading into – Twickenham, with 75,000 bellowing people inside. I don't know if I looked around but I was bouncing with nervous energy during the national anthems. I just tried to keep on top of everything, calm myself down and look as if I was in control. But, in truth, I had never heard such a loud crowd before."

1871 ENGLAND TEAM

Film Strip

85

# ENGLAND firsts

# 1871

## FIRST

### England international

The RFU didn't have to wait long for their first ever sporting international following its founding in January 1871.

In fact, just two months after those pivotal meetings in the Pall Mall Restaurant, England were invited to face Scotland at Raeburn Place, Edinburgh on March 27.

The game was slightly different to the one we recognise today, as both teams had 20 players with 13 forwards and seven backs.

England travelled up for the match the day before, sleeping in third-class on the train and paying their own expenses

However, they had no real reward for their efforts as Scotland won by one goal to nil, after W. Cross converted Angus Buchanan's try.

England also scored a try, through R. H. Birkett, but England captain F. Stokes, missed the place kick and because tries did not count at the time, the home side were the victors.

excepting the ribald boys outside); and nothing unfitted for the presence of sisters or wives All was good humour and cheerful, unaffected gaiety, and there could be no mistake concerning the social position of the promoters and chief actors of the day. If the opening meeting of the London Athletic Club be a fair sample of the gatherings which are to follow, its authorities have rendered a substantial public service in establishing one more healthy outdoor entertainment which people of both sexes can look at and enjoy."

#### FOOTBALL MATCH BETWEEN ENGLAND AND SCOTLAND.

On Monday the great football match, "England versus Scotland," was played at Edinburgh in the presence of a large number of spectators. The twenties pitted against each other were the representatives of the best clubs in the two countries. The game was keenly contested, and during the first fifty minutes both sides touched down and were equal. After changing sides, the Scotch twenty invaded the quarters of the English and became entitled to a try. The kick off resulted in a goal being obtained. The English twenty afterwards got a try, but failed to obtain a goal. After a hard struggle the Scotch team again got a touch down in the English ground, but did not succeed in obtaining a goal with their try. Time being then up, the Scotch were declared the winners by a goal and a touch down

#### LONDON SWIMMING CLUB'S ATHLETIC SPORTS.

The athletic sports of this club will be held at the Tufnell-Park Cricket-Grounds, Holloway, on Saturday, April 15, when the programme will consist of 100-Yards Handicap Flat Race, Quarter-of-a-Mile Handicap Flat Race, and a Ten-Miles Handicap Flat Race. The 100-yards race will be confined to members, and the ten-miles race and quarter-mile will be open to all gentlemen amateurs. Mr. Page, the proprietor, having made a new path round his grounds, every facility will be offered to the gentlemen composing the ... and hounds to try

## FIRST

## International caps

These caps were awarded to players who took part in the first ever rugby international in 1871. The England cap, *left*, belonged to A.G. Guillemard. He was Old Rugbeian, as was half of the English team in this match. Guillemard was a founding member of the RFU and one of rugby's strongest advocates in the early days.

The Scotland cap, *below*, belonged to J.W. Arthur. Arthur was born in Glasgow and played for Glasgow Academicals for seven seasons, as well as representing his country twice. Arthur was one of the Scottish club representatives that challenged England to the match.

## FIRST

## England shirt

This is the shirt worn by J. H. Clayton of Liverpool during England's inaugural meeting with Scotland. Clayton was one of the 10 Old Rugbeians in the first English international side.

He was also one of 13 England players in that first game who would never represent their country again.

The white jersey with a red rose may have been adopted by England as a tribute to the colours worn at Rugby School but a wide range of theories exist as to why England adopted their famous uniform.

# 1910

## FIRST

### England game to be held at Twickenham

England enjoyed a winning start at Twickenham in their first match at what was to become 'HQ'.

Wales were beaten 11-6 on January 15, 1910, as the first Five Nations Championship was contested. France had just joined the tournament, which had previously been known as the Home Nations Championship.

Fred Chapman scored a try in the first minute, while Cornishman Barney Solomon went over later in the game. Tom Evans got the sole Welsh try. It was the first Red Rose victory over the Principality in 12 years.

England went on win the title unbeaten, a 0-0 draw with Ireland preventing a Grand Slam.

Fred Chapman, *left*, got England off to a flying start against Wales in 1910 and, *top*, the 15 Englishmen who made history at Twickenham that day. *Above*: The matchday programme shows the line-up

# 1913

The first Grand Slam-winning England team line up ahead of their 20-0 victory over France and, *right*, action from the game in which Vincent Coates scored a hat-trick

## English Grand Slam

A first English Grand Slam was achieved in 1913 in the fourth championship that included France.

A measly four points were conceded as the title was won in some style.

In England's first game on January 18, Wales were beaten 12-0 in Cardiff with tries from winger Vincent Coates and forward Cherry Pillman. John Greenwood kicked one conversion and Ronald Poulton-Palmer, a centre, slotted a drop-goal.

A week later, the points were garnered by the same men as France were defeated 20-0. Coates scored a hat-trick, Pillman a brace and the final try went to Poulton-Palmer. Greenwood again managed a single conversion.

Coates continued his rich vein of form with two tries as Ireland were handed a 15-5 reverse in Dublin. Pillman also went over the line, as did forward John Ritson. Greenwood kicked a penalty, while Ireland's sole score was a drop-goal by fly-half Dickie Lloyd.

The Calcutta Cup, Triple Crown and Grand Slam was sealed with a narrow 3-0 victory over the Scots. The only try went to the brilliantly-named prop Bruno Brown in front of 25,000 people at Twickenham.

England's winning captain was Norman Wodehouse, who later went on to serve as a gunnery officer at the Battle of Jutland, and attained the rank of Vice-Admiral before being lost at sea after a U-boat attack during the Second World War in July 1941, while commanding a convoy from South Africa.

Poulton-Palmer, an attacking three-quarter, was killed by a sniper's bullet in May 1915 during the First World War, aged 25.

Coates, who finished the championship with six tries, was a Captain in the Army's Medical Corps and was awarded the Military Cross during the Battle of the Somme. He died, aged 45, in 1934 after falling from a train in Maidenhead.

## Stoop's Scrapbook

A deep thinker of the game he devoted much of his life to, it is only natural that Adrian Stoop would document his rise through the rugby ranks.

From his time at Rugby School and Oxford University, to captaining both club and country, Stoop preserved those treasured memories in this scrapbook, which now forms part of the impressive collection of memorabilia at the World Rugby Museum located in the East Stand at Twickenham.

# FIRST

## Twickenham captain

Adrian Stoop was England's first Twickenham captain when they played Wales in 1910. However, his rugby legacy goes far beyond those 80 minutes.

Stoop was an early England and Harlequins legend, playing 15 times for his country as well as over 150 appearances for Harlequins.

He helped to make the London side the strongest club in the country and also popularised the idea of having designated scrum-halves and fly-halves, rather than interchanging players in those two positions.

This change allowed England and Harlequins to dominate, and although he was seriously injured while fighting in World War I, he made a full recovery and played his last match for Harlequins, aged 56.

Their home ground, Twickenham Stoop – less than a mile from Twickenham – is named after him.

### Sewn into history

This is Adrian Stoop's Rugby School cap from Steel House, 1899. The writing inside represents the teams that Steel House played and the dates of the games. This practice of sewing in the names of the opposition teams went on until the start of World War I.

# FIRST

## Match to be broadcast

England's opening Five Nations match in January 1927 against Wales was the first sporting event to be broadcast live on radio in Britain. Former Harlequins captain Teddy Wakelam was the main commentator. A graphic had been published in that week's Radio Times which divided the pitch into numbered squares. While Wakelam described the play at Twickenham, a voice in the background identified the square the play was happening in. It has been claimed that the phrase 'back to square one' originated from this practice.

# FIRST

## Kick at Twickenham

GV Carey, who went on to be headmaster of Eastbourne College, was the first man to kick-off at Twickenham when the inaugural match at the new ground took place between Harlequins and Richmond on October 2, 1909. In front of an estimated crowd of between 2,000 and 3,500, Carey's kick failed to travel the required distance, leading to the first scrum.

# FIRST

## Black player

The first black player to represent England was Salford-born James Peters. The son of a Jamaican father and Shropshire mother, Peters was orphaned as a child. He played for Bristol and Plymouth and represented England twice in 1907, against Scotland and France, scoring a try in the French encounter. Peters later played rugby league for Barrow and St Helens.

# FIRST

## Try at Twickenham

The first England try at Twickenham was scored by Fred Chapman inside the first minute of an 11-6 victory over Wales in 1910.

# FIRST

## Twickenham streaker

Michael O'Brien, a 25-year-old Australian, was the first known streaker at a major sporting event when he ran onto the Twickenham pitch during an England v France Five Nations match in March 1974. A policeman covered his modesty with a strategically-placed helmet. However, Erica Roe remains the most famous Twickenham streaker, thanks to her joyful run across the pitch when England played Australia in January 1982.

## FIRST

### Televised match

The first televised rugby international was the Calcutta Cup match of 1938 at Twickenham, which Scotland won 21-16 to clinch the championship. Teddy Wakelam, the radio pioneer of 1927, was again the chosen commentator.

## FIRST

### England player to be sent off

Mike Burton, *left*, was the first England player to be sent off. He was dismissed for a late tackle on Australian winger Doug Osbourne just three minutes into a Test in 1975 that came to be known as the 'Battle of Brisbane'. He was only the third player to be sent off in international rugby.

## FIRST

### England coach

Don White was England's first appointed coach, serving in the role between 1969 and 1971. A prop and Northampton stalwart who made 448 appearances for his club, he won 14 caps for his country before moving into coaching. In his first game in charge, he oversaw England's first victory over South Africa.

## FIRST

### Replacement

Tim Dalton, then 28, was the first England replacement, earning his only cap when coming on for Keith Field in an 8-3 Calcutta Cup victory at Twickenham in March 1969. David Duckham scored two tries in the win.

## A. OBOLENSKY

### POSITION: WING THREE-QUARTERS
### VS NEW ZEALAND, JANUARY 4, 1936

Prince Alexander Sergeevich Obolensky arrived in England from Russia with his family in 1917 and had a brief but glorious England career before tragedy struck. After excelling at rugby at Trent College and Oxford University, he was selected for England against the All Blacks at Twickenham and shone on his debut, scoring two stunning tries that left the crowd in awe of his speed and side-step.

He only played three further games for England but the winger was a crowd favourite, especially when it was revealed that his performances were fuelled by a pre-match meal of oysters and champagne. However, despite escaping the Russian Revolution, bad luck would catch up with Prince Obolensky in March 1940, when he died – aged just 24 – following a training accident while on duty with the RAF.

## P. WINTERBOTTOM

### POSITION: FLANKER
### VS AUSTRALIA, JAN 2, 1982

The international career of one of England's greatest ever back-row forwards began with a fine, narrow victory over Australia. The match was the start of an 11-year, 58-cap England career but is perhaps best remember for the topless intervention of Erica Roe, who streaked across the the Twickenham turf during the match.

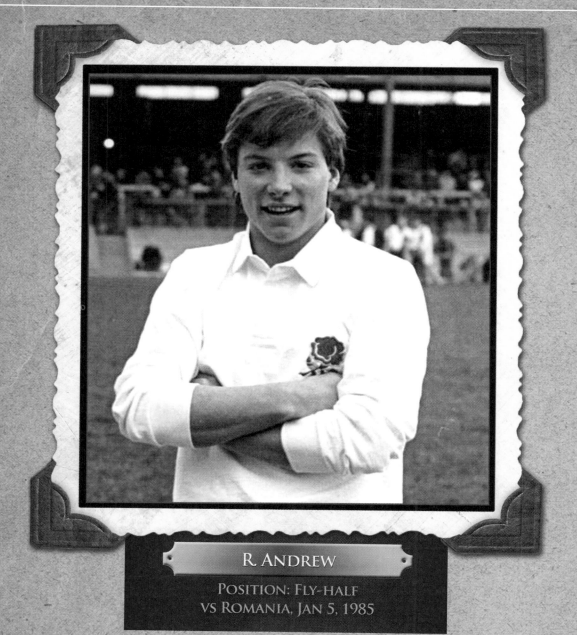

## R. ANDREW

### POSITION: FLY-HALF
### VS ROMANIA, JAN 5, 1985

Rob Andrew's 71-cap career started in glorious style against Romania in 1985. Barely a minute into the match, he kicked a drop-goal as England went on to win 22-15 at Twickenham. It was the start of an international career that brought three Grand Slams as well as a Rugby World Cup final place and a host of other sensational rugby memories.

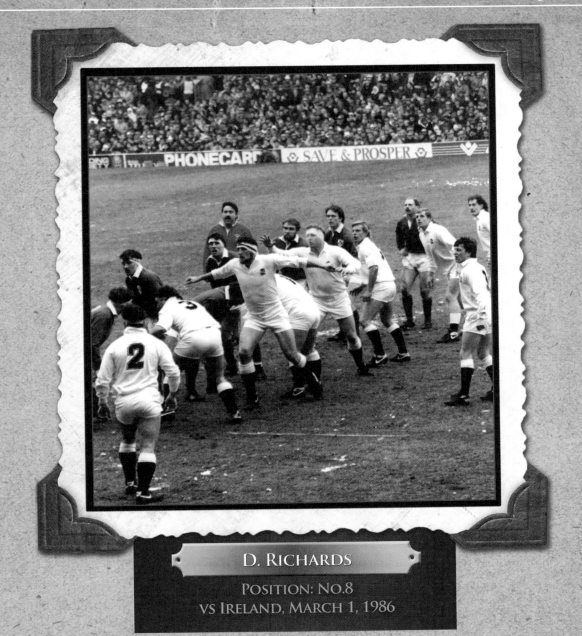

## D. RICHARDS

POSITION: NO.8
VS IRELAND, MARCH 1, 1986

Dean Richards may have looked scruffy on the pitch but there have been fewer smarter No.8s in rugby history. Against Ireland in a tetchy, tight Five Nations game in March 1986, he made his debut and scored two tries as England won by five points. It was the start of 48 caps for Richards as he went on to cement himself as an indispensable member of England's pack in the '80s and early '90s.

## J. GUSCOTT

### POSITION: CENTRE
### VS ROMANIA, MAY 13, 1989

A graceful hat-trick on his debut; Jeremy Guscott
started as he meant to go on. The Bath centre can
barely have dreamt that his international career would
get off to such a glorious beginning as England routed
Romania in Bucharest. His three tries were the start of a
65-match England career and he was to go on to score a
further 27 tries for his country, ensuring he goes down
in history as a genuine England great.

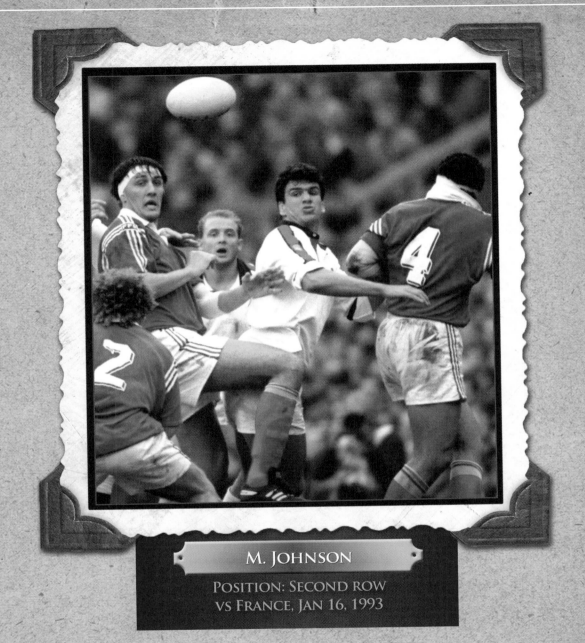

## M. JOHNSON

### POSITION: SECOND ROW
### VS FRANCE, JAN 16, 1993

Even the greatest of Test careers can have bizarre beginnings. Martin Johnson was a last-gasp choice for England's match against France in January 1993 because of a late injury to Wade Dooley. When Johnson arrived at Twickenham, he barely knew the line-out drills and had to have a rushed practice to try and help him out. However, he shrugged off all the drama and went on to play superbly in a narrow 16-15 win over Les Bleus. Perhaps the finest England Test career of them all was finally underway.

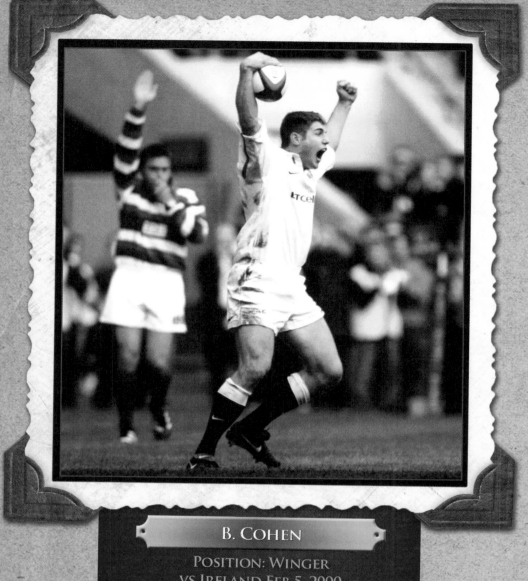

## B. COHEN

### POSITION: WINGER
### VS IRELAND FEB 5, 2000

England trounced Ireland 50-18 at Twickenham as Ben Cohen showed he was more than capable at mixing it with the best on the world stage. The powerful winger, who was virtually unstoppable when he got up to full speed, scored twice on his international debut and he went on to become a member of the England side that won the Rugby World Cup in 2003. He eventually retired with a fantastic international scoring record of 31 tries from 57 appearances.

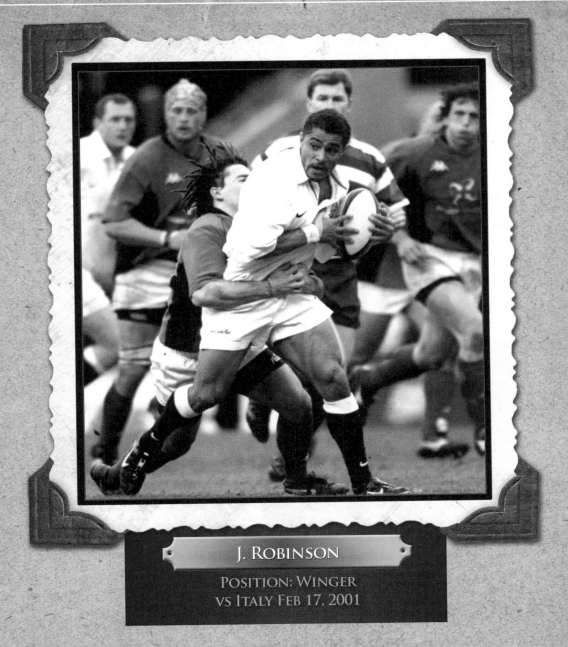

## J. ROBINSON

### POSITION: WINGER
### VS ITALY FEB 17, 2001

There can have been fewer quicker and more glorious rises through the rugby union ranks than that of 'Billy Whizz'. Jason Robinson was a rugby league legend in 2000 when he shocked the sporting world by converting codes, joining Sale Sharks. He made his domestic debut in November against Coventry and just three months later he was selected by Clive Woodward, coming off the bench as England comfortably beat Italy at Twickenham. He may not have scored in his first match but his arrival in the 15-man code was one of the final pieces in what turned into the 2003 Rugby World Cup-winning jigsaw.

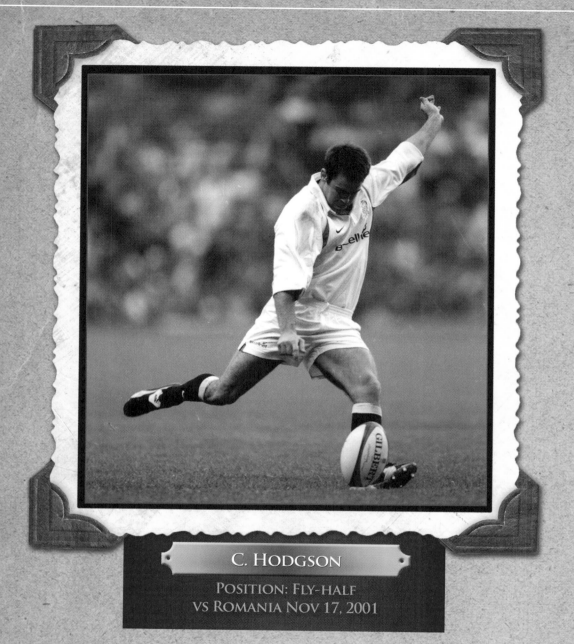

## C. HODGSON

### POSITION: FLY-HALF
### VS ROMANIA NOV 17, 2001

Scoring 44 points for your country in any game would be something to remember. To do it on your debut takes the achievement to an entirely different level and that is what Charlie Hodgson did in 2001. Romania may not have been the strongest opposition as England wracked up an incredible 134-0 win, but Hodgson's vision and composure, along with his points haul, means his debut is comfortably one of the finest in international history.

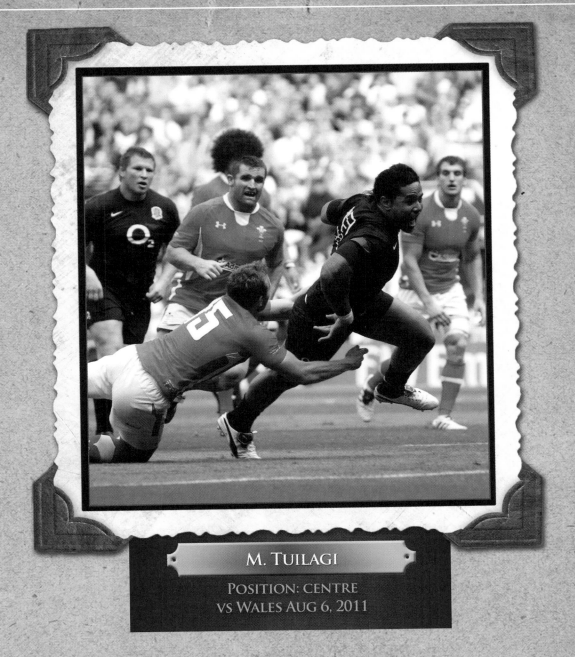

## M. TUILAGI

### POSITION: CENTRE
### VS WALES AUG 6, 2011

England beat Wales in this World Cup warm-up match with Tuilagi underlining exactly why Martin Johnson had selected him for the side. Tuilagi capped off his debut with a stunning powerful try, barging through the Welsh defence and holding off three defenders to finish under the posts.

# Brothers in arms

Incredibly, 28 sets of brothers have played for England and, of that group, 12 pairs of brothers have entered the field of battle side by side in the same match.

Reginald and Louis Birkett started the trend when England faced Scotland in Edinburgh on March 8, 1875.

The most frequent pairing have been the popular Underwood duo who were on the same side an incredible 19 times. The brothers played together at Leicester and featured on opposite wings for England, starting on November 14, 1992 when England beat South Africa 33-16 at Twickenham.

## Brothers who have played together for England

- Reginald and Louis Birkett
- John and Harry Graham
- Temple and Charles Gurdon
- Robert and James Hunt
- Fred and Francis Byrne
- Frank and Percy Stout
- James and Joseph Davidson
- Adrian and Tim Stoop
- Harold and Arthur Wheatley
- Rory and Tony Underwood
- Delon and Steffon Armitage
- Ben and Tom Youngs

# MY ENGLAND
## BEN YOUNGS

"I'll stand beside him at the anthem. He's my brother. I want to be shoulder to shoulder with him. It's going to be a very, very special moment. To play alongside my brother in an England shirt at Twickenham, is going to be a pretty amazing feeling. I'll try to feed off that emotion and energy and try to put it into my performance."

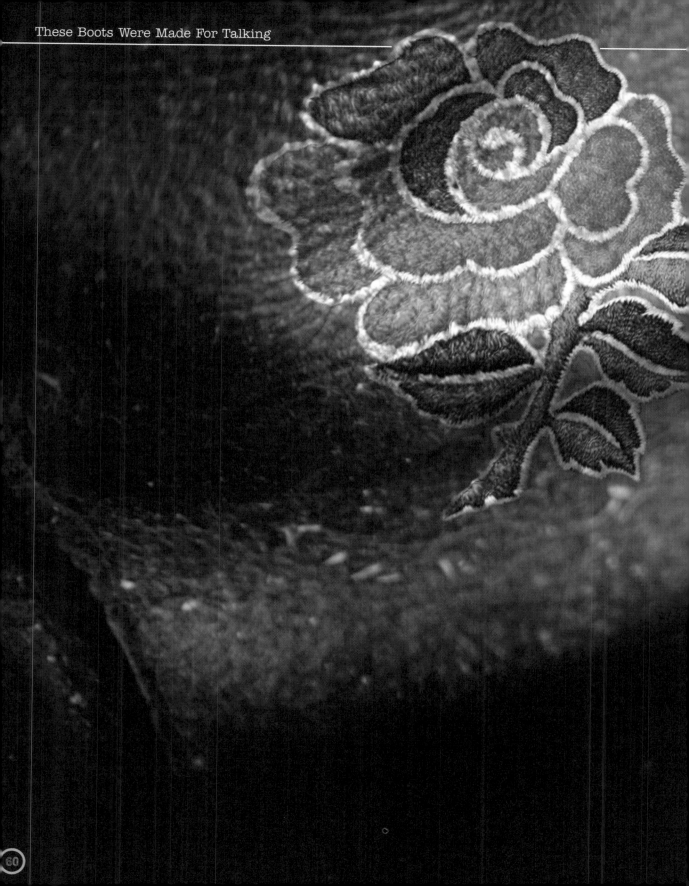

# THESE Boots WERE MADE FOR Talking

While fundamentally a hands-on sport, goal kicking has become one of the most important aspects of rugby, as games are frequently decided by penalties and conversions. Fortunately, England have produced some of the world's best kicking talent, and continue to do so.

"YOU HAVE TO GET IT RIGHT, WEEK IN, WEEK OUT. I'M NOT TALKING ABOUT YOUR BEST. EVERY TEAM CAN DO THAT. I'M TALKING ABOUT YOUR WORST, WHEN YOUR WORST IS STILL A SEVEN-OUT-OF-TEN. CONSISTENT EXCELLENCE IS ABOUT YOUR BOTTOM LINE."

- Jonny Wilkinson

# The whole world at his feet

When an 18-year-old – one of England's youngest-ever internationals – replaced Mike Catt during England's Five Nations victory over Ireland at Twickenham on April 4, 1998, few of the 75,000 present could have imagined that they were witnessing the birth of a legend.

Some 13 years, 91 England caps (plus six more for the British and Irish Lions), 1,246 international points and one World Cup winners' medal later, and that legend was complete.

The 18 year old was Jonathan Peter Wilkinson who would become England's all-time leading points scorer and unquestionably the finest fly-half of his, and perhaps any other, generation.

Of those 1,246 points, Wilkinson will of course be forever associated with just three of them; the last-gasp drop-goal that won England the Rugby World Cup in Sydney in 2003.

A naturally left-footed kicker, Wilkinson coolly slotted Matt Dawson's pinpoint pass through the posts with his 'wrong' foot and into the crowd, a moment he had waited for his entire life and a moment he had trained for almost as long.

Disciplined, calm, clear-headed, accurate

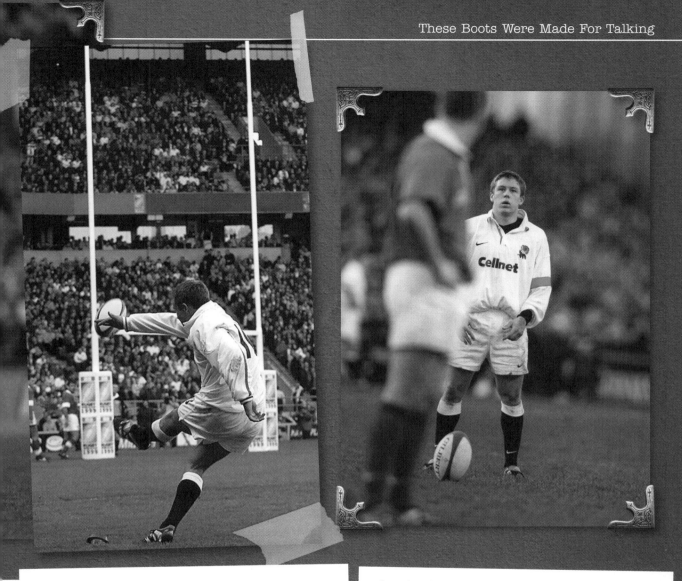

and deadly; the drop-goal perfectly encapsulated Wilkinson's England performances and rugby philosophy.

His quiet and respectful demeanour in everyday life gave way to a rugby force of nature when he pulled on an England shirt, and his work ethic often left new team-mates staggered as he set about almost single-handedly redesigning the role of the modern fly-half.

In the past, most international No.10s left the hard tackling to the forwards, but Wilkinson screamed and shuddered into contact as if he were the world's best flanker.

His desire for perfection and his desire to never let his team-mates down meant he knew no other way, and that drop-goal in Sydney brought him

the plaudits and attention that the thousands of hours of behind-closed-doors practice deserved.

However, few English sports stars have been so feted but also so uncomfortable with the attention their efforts received. Wilkinson felt that he was always just one of a starting XV, or a matchday squad of 22 or a World Cup squad of 30. It was arguably his finest trait – and there were many to choose from.

The frightening aspect about Wilkinson's international career is that he could potentially have played another 40 Tests for England and scored another 500 points if he had not been so affected by injury.

Following his heroics in Sydney, he did not

play for England again until the 2007 Six Nations match against Scotland – a hiatus of over a 1,000 days – due to knee, kidney, shoulder and arm injuries.

However, in that Calcutta Cup game he scored a record 27 points and was man of the match, underlining again that no matter the circumstances or his injury record, Wilkinson could still drive England to victory.

Further World Cups followed in 2007 and 2011 but England could not repeat the magic of 2003 – despite being beaten finalists in 2007 –

and Wilkinson retired from England duty in December 2011 so he could concentrate on his domestic career with French side Toulon, who he had joined in 2009 from Newcastle Falcons.

His England career may have been halted and set back by injuries, but Wilkinson's achievements, work ethic, respect for opponents and his willingness to help out those team-mates around him – in matches and in practice – means he holds a very special place in the hearts and history of English rugby. Consistent excellence indeed.

"I CONSIDER MYSELF REALLY LUCKY TO HAVE HAD HIM AS A PLAYER. I FIRST CAPPED HIM AS AN 18-YEAR-OLD. PEOPLE TALK ABOUT A MODEL PROFESSIONAL; WELL, HE WAS THE MODEL MODEL. HE WAS IMMENSE IN EVERY WAY."

- Clive Woodward

### Leading Conversion Table

| | | | | |
|---|---|---|---|---|
| 1 | D Carter | NZ | 2003-2012 | 245 |
| 2 | R O'Gara | Ire/Lions | 2000-2013 | 176 |
| 3 | J Wilkinson | Eng/Lions | 1998-2011 | 169 |
| - | A Mehrtens | NZ | 1995-2004 | 169 |
| 5 | S Jones | Wales/Lions | 1998-2011 | 160 |

# Following in Jonny's footsteps

### Top Penalty Takers

| | | | | |
|---|---|---|---|---|
| 1 | J Wilkinson | Eng/Lions | 1998-2011 | 255 |
| 2 | N Jenkins | Wales/Lions | 1991-2002 | 248 |
| 3 | D Carter | NZ | 2003-2012 | 244 |
| 4 | D Dominguez | Arg/Italy | 1989-2003 | 213 |
| 5 | R O'Gara | Ire/Lions | 2000-2013 | 202 |

### Leading Drop-goal Scorers

| | | | | |
|---|---|---|---|---|
| 1 | J Wilkinson | Eng/Lions | 1998-2011 | 36 |
| 2 | H Porta | Arg/Sth Am | 1971-1990 | 28 |
| 3 | R Andrew | Eng/Lions | 1985-1997 | 23 |
| 4 | D Dominguez | Arg/Italy | 1989-2003 | 20 |
| 5 | N Botha | SA | 1980-1992 | 18 |

Jonny Wilkinson's prolonged absences from the England team due to injury meant that when he did retire from international duty in 2011, his potential 'successors' had already seen plenty of action at Twickenham and beyond.

Paul Grayson, Andy Goode, Charlie Hodgson, Dave Walder, Olly Barkley, Danny Cipriani, Alex King and Shane Geraghty all had designs on the No.10 shirt at one time or another, but Toby Flood has consistently been the fly-half to turn to.

Over 50 caps for England during an international career that began in 2006 speaks for itself.

Flood is only too aware that his impact on the national side has often been as a result of Wilkinson's unavailability, but the Leicester Tigers man has never felt overshadowed by his fellow fly-half.

In fact, the national side often accommodated both men, with Flood starting at inside centre.

As well as featuring alongside each other for England, Flood also lined up with Wilkinson at Newcastle Falcons, and he feels fortunate to have played with someone who always led by example.

He said: "I learned from a young age about Jonny's work ethic.

"Your eyes are taken to the back of your head when you realised what he was prepared to go though to achieve what he wanted to do.

"He was peerless during my time at Newcastle and different to anything else that was going on.

"Seeing a guy like that who was at the top of his game, made me realise that, as an 18-year-old coming into that side, I had to raise my game.

"When I was 16 or 17 and he was top of the world, he had a huge influence. He could have led a celebratory lifestyle, but he just shut up shop and got on with his day job. As a younger man who saw what he was doing, it made you put in the same amount of training. You were always trying to get to his level.

"I never saw it as a competition, I thought it was always a chance for me to learn from somebody who was outstanding."

And just as Wilkinson had to watch over his shoulder when Flood underlined his England staying power, Flood has also had to do the same with the emergence of Owen Farrell, another No.10 who seems destined to feature for the national side for some considerable time.

Farrell's calm and commanding performances for England have provoked comparisons with no lesser player than Wilkinson himself but, typically, the England legend has been the first person to play down any similarities.

Wilkinson said: "I know people are making comparisons, but forget about me.

"Owen's writing his own story now and doing it very well.

"What sets the best apart is that they don't just do all the obvious stuff for all to see, such as the big hits, the clever passes and the crucial kicks. It's the other stuff that only a player can fully appreciate.

"I'm talking about making a nine-out-of-ten tackle, getting back on to your feet and making another tackle, say an eight-out-of-ten, within seconds, getting up again, making a third tackle in the space of a couple of minutes, then receiving the ball and making the right decision to set off an attack, before, moments later, placing the ball down and preparing to kick what could be three crucial points. That requires a mental toughness that

"JONNY WAS AN AMAZING PLAYER AND STILL IS. JUST EVEN TO BE TALKED ABOUT IN THE SAME SENTENCE AS HIM IS PRETTY GOOD. I WAS LUCKY ENOUGH TO BE IN FRANCE WHEN MY DAD WAS PLAYING AT THE 2007 WORLD CUP AND WAS ABLE TO WATCH JONNY DOING KICKING SESSIONS. I TOOK A LOT FROM IT. JONNY SHOWED HOW MUCH HARD WORK WAS PUT IN TO BEING A TOP PLAYER.

- Owen Farrell

I can see in Owen, and strong leadership."

Wilkinson clearly feels confident about the depth of choice England have at fly-half and he believes that Flood, Farrell and Gloucester's Freddie Burns are all going to fight each other for the No.10 jersey for some considerable time.

"The key is to continue what they are doing, which is a relentless pursuit of precision of execution and consistency, and the guys do that fabulously, which is why they're not throw-away names now," he added.

"You've got guys who are stepping up. They are pushing each other. Whoever has that jersey has got it because they have had to push their level above what the other guys are doing."

## Boots down the years

The origins of rugby footwear can loosely be traced back to 1526 when Henry VIII called for a pair of leather football boots.

However, it wasn't until the late 1800s before players were able to wear something resembling a rugby boot. These were usually walking or working boots, or even hobnail boots which would come with nails or studs protruding.

By the time the sports divided into rugby and football, the structure of the boot incorporated metal tips as a way for players to inflict more pain on opponents via the acceptable practice of 'hacking' at each other's legs.

Projecting nails or iron plates were eventually outlawed in 1889 and more safety measures were introduced around the time of England's first ever international match at Twickenham in 1910. These changes instructed the use of a cylindrical stud no less than ¾ inch in diameter and no longer than half the diameter long, and fixed to the sole by four nails.

More stud changes came in 1926 when the construction had to be leather, circular and fixed by at least three nails. Rubber was included in 1948, aluminium in 1953 and, a year later, approved plastics.

Currently, rugby requires an approved rugby boot with studs that carry the IRB marking which can be used for both rugby union and rugby league.

### Lasting impression

These boots were first worn in the 1900s as the popularity of rugby grew. The design was largely unchanged for over half a century.

### Treading carefully

Black leather, white laces and less studs were put on these 1920s boots.

## Different boot for different positions

Traditional rugby boots are very similar to football boots, the one notable exception being the high cut designed to provide extra ankle support. These were used more prominently by the forwards but nowadays more players, backs in particular, prefer to use football style boots as the lower cut affords them more mobility.

### Noticeably All Black

A 1924 New Zealand black leather, miniature pair of rugby boots.

### Heeling properties

A brown leather heel and moulded studs were incorporated into this design.

### Boom of the branded boot

As the game entered the '70s, boot makers became more savvy with the world of marketing and so began to engineer their products in a way which made them instantly recognisable – such as these adidas 3-Stripe specimens. They were intended for use by forwards, with extra ankle support factored into the design.

ENGLAND
RUGBY

# TWICKENHAM TREASURES

## Prized possessions inside the England vault

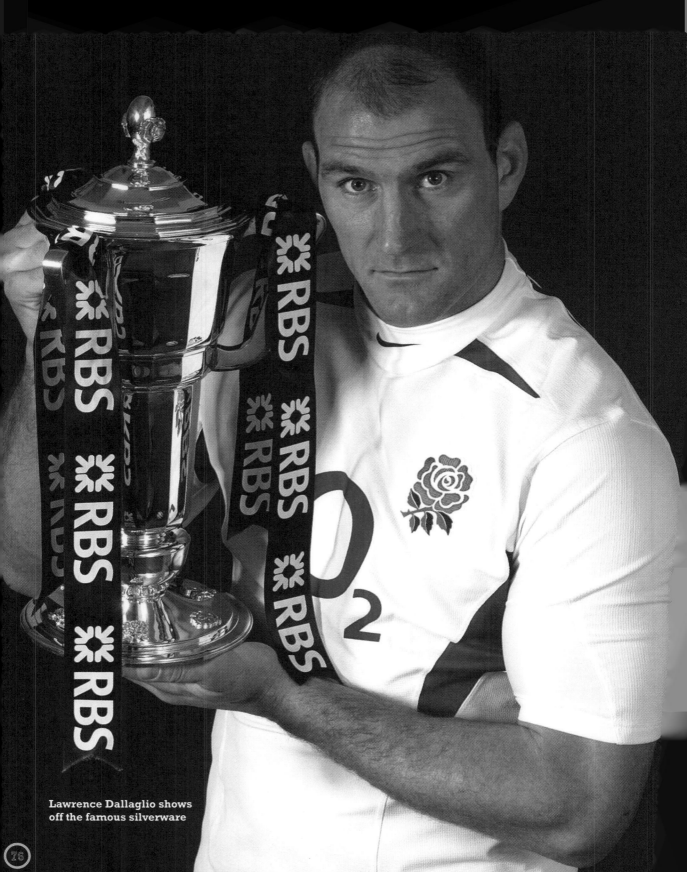

Lawrence Dallaglio shows
off the famous silverware

# The Six Nations

The Six Nations began life as the Home Nations Championship, which was first played in 1883.

Before then, matches between the 'home nations' – England, Ireland, Scotland and Wales – had been informal, sporadic affairs with no permanently set fixtures or long-term organisation.

Beating the three other sides in the annual event allowed a country to boast that they had won the 'Triple Crown', which is a tradition that remains to this day.

Although winning the Triple Crown is the oldest accolade in the tournament, no actual trophy was awarded for the feat until 2006.

In 1910, France joined the competition and the phrase 'Five Nations Championship' was coined as a better name for the tournament.

England won the inaugural Five Nations Championship while Wales went one better the year after as they claimed the first 'Grand Slam'.

The tournament was halted due to World War I but when hostilities stopped, it was resumed in 1920.

Eleven years later, France were barred from the competition because of the mismanagement of their national side and the fact that several players had allegedly been paid at club level, thus breaking the sport's amateur rules.

The tournament then continued in its previous four-side format until 1939 when France were due to be reintroduced, but the arrival of World War II put another halt on the event until it restarted in 1947.

No actual trophy was given for winning the Five Nations Championship until 1993 when France were victorious.

Scotland were the last side to lift the Five Nations Championship trophy in 1999 as Italy expanded the competition to the Six Nations in 2000.

As for the trophy itself, it is made from sterling silver, was designed by James Brent-Ward and was made by London silversmith company William Comyns.

Over the years, the trophy has been repeatedly filled with champagne and has now been lined with 22 carat gold to stop the champagne from damaging the inside.

The base of the trophy contains the emblem of all six competing nations, has 15 sides to represent each player as well as three handles to represent the referee and both touch judges.

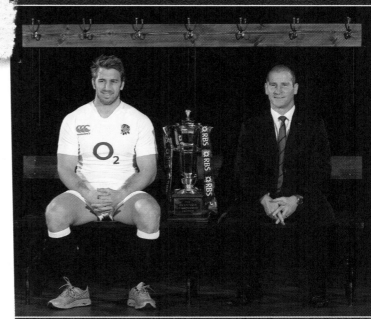

England captain Chris Robshaw and head coach Stuart Lancaster at the launch of the 2013 RBS 6 Nations

| | ENG | FRA | IRE | ITA | SCO | WAL |
|---|---|---|---|---|---|---|
| Tournaments | 117 | 84 | 119 | 14 | 119 | 119 |
| ▼ Outright Wins (Shared Wins) ▼ | | | | | | |
| Home Nations | 5 (4) | - | 4 (3) | - | 9 (2) | 7 (4) |
| Five Nations | 17 (6) | 12 (8) | 6 (5) | - | 5 (6) | 15 (8) |
| Six Nations | 4 | 5 | 1 | 0 | 0 | 4 |
| Overall | 26 (10) | 17 (8) | 11 (9) | 0 (0) | 14 (8) | 26 (12) |
| Grand Slams | 12 | 9 | 2 | 0 | 3 | 11 |
| Triple Crowns | 23 | N/A | 10 | N/A | 10 | 20 |

England have achieved Grand Slam glory on 12 occasions. Here we look back at some of their more recent successes...

# 1991 Grand Slam

After the bitter disappointment of 1990, there was a fierce determination among the England squad to end the 11-year wait for a Five Nations title. Grand Slam glory was to be theirs, but it was a hard-won achievement.

The opening fixture was in Cardiff, where England had not won since 1963. Coach Geoff Cooke ensured his side was not intimidated by the natives by booking them into a city centre hotel overlooking the old Arms Park. Welsh anthems were played over the loudspeaker during training sessions in the days before the match and when they drove over the Severn Bridge.

In a grim struggle decided up front, England won with something to spare. Simon Hodgkinson kicked a then-world record seven penalties while a late Mike Teague try sealed a 25-6 victory, which removed one psychological block.

Scotland were then beaten 21-12 at Twickenham, with Nigel Heslop scoring the only try and Hodgkinson kicking another 17 points.

The trip to Dublin provided another tough test and, deep into the second half, there was little to choose between the sides, but late scores for Teague and Rory Underwood allowed England to pull away to a 16-7 victory. It was all set up for a Grand Slam showdown against the French.

The quality of the contest matched the billing »

of the occasion. England took an early lead through a Hodgkinson penalty but when the full-back missed another penalty attempt, they were stunned as France, inspired by Serge Blanco, eschewed a regulation 22-metre drop-out and surged from one end of the field to the other, culminating in Philippe Saint-Andre's try of the century.

England calmly regrouped and built an 18-6 interval lead, featuring a joyous score for Rory Underwood. France came back in the second half with further tries for Didier Camberabero and Frank Mesnel but England held on for a 21-19 victory that thrilled the home crowd.

This was the only time England used the same 15 players for an entire Championship, a victory built by the formidable forward line of Jason Leonard, Brian Moore, Jeff Probyn, Wade Dooley, Paul Ackford, Mike Teague, Peter Winterbottom and Dean Richards.

# 1992 Grand Slam

After grinding their way to the Grand Slam in 1991, it was a much more expansive England who repeated the feat 12 months later.

Buoyed by reaching the World Cup final at home the previous autumn, Will Carling's men attacked the Five Nations with brio, winning all their matches by comfortable margins.

Scotland were first up at Murrayfield and England triumphed 25-7 with tries from Dewi Morris and Rory Underwood. Jonathan Webb kicked 14 points and Jeremy Guscott popped over a drop-goal.

Two weeks later, Ireland were comprehensively beaten 38-9 at Twickenham as six tries were scored courtesy of Guscott, Morris, Simon Halliday, Rory Underwood and two from Webb, who contributed 22 points in all.

Then it was the cauldron of Parc des Princes but England enjoyed one of their most comfortable victories in Paris as they »

>> repeatedly split asunder the French defence. Morris, Webb and Rory Underwood all crossed the line again, while a penalty try was also awarded as France lost their discipline and had two men sent off. England won 31-13.

Wales were the opposition as England went for back-to-back Grand Slams and they reached their goal in fine style, winning 24-0. Captain Carling, Wade Dooley and Micky Skinner were the try scorers and Webb completed an excellent personal tournament with another 12 points.

England's total of 15 tries was a record for a side that produced some thrilling and compelling rugby in the 1992 tournament.

# 1995 Grand Slam

The 1995 Grand Slam was one of the last hurrahs for the wonderful England team of the early 1990s that swept through three Five Nations tournaments, reached the 1991 Rugby World Cup final and the semi-final four years later.

The third of these Slams began with a 20-8 victory in Dublin, achieved with tries from skipper Will Carling, Ben Clarke and Tony Underwood.

France were next at Twickenham. In the build-up, England hooker Brian Moore stirred things up nicely by referring to the French team as "15 Eric Cantonas" at a time when their compatriot was banned from football for assaulting a rival supporter.

There was little drama on the field as England won 31-10 with two tries from Tony Underwood »

>> and one from Jeremy Guscott. It was the biggest English victory over France for 48 years.

Then it was off to Cardiff where the English had only won once since 1963. It proved to be a comfortable enough afternoon as a brace for the other Underwood – Rory – and a try from Victor Ubogu helped the Red Rose to a 23-9 success.

As Scotland won in Paris on the same day, the Calcutta Cup contest at Twickenham would be a Grand Slam decider, five years after the Scots emerged victorious in the same situation at Murrayfield.

On this occasion, England would prevail, easing to a 24-12 victory with all the points coming from the boot of Rob Andrew, who kicked seven penalties and a drop-goal.

As in 1991, the England team remained unchanged throughout the competition.

## MY ENGLAND
### WILL CARLING

"They say you never forget your first time and they are right. The first Grand Slam remains one of my dearest memories. The Grand Slam means an awful lot to England supporters and as a player you feel priveliged to have been a part of it; to have helped give the supporters all over the country something to celebrate."

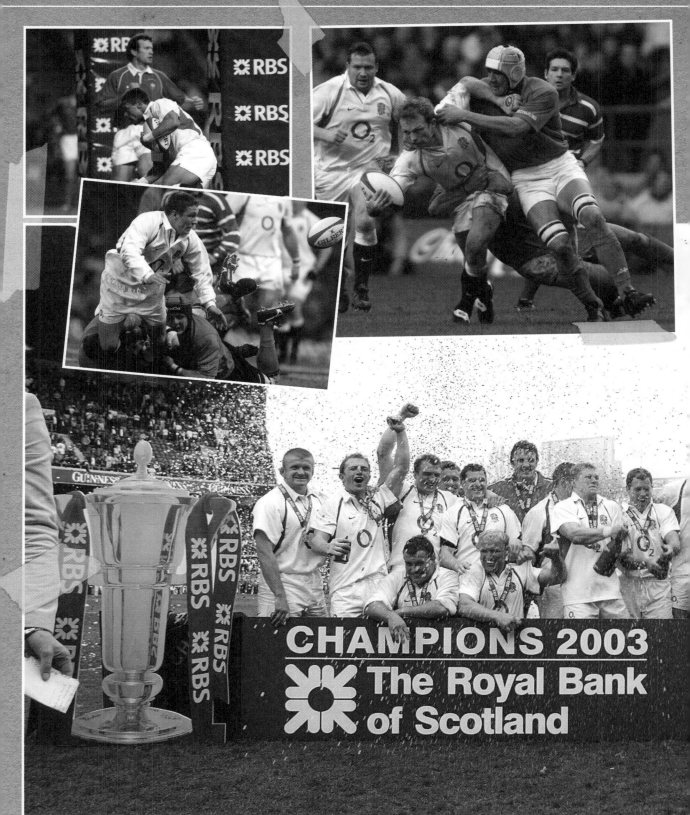

CHAMPIONS 2003
The Royal Bank
of Scotland

# 2003 Grand Slam

After three agonising near-misses in the previous four seasons, the 2003 Grand Slam was a thrilling release for an outstanding England side and set them up perfectly for World Cup glory later in the year.

The tournament began against France at Twickenham but hearts were heavy as Harlequins youngster Nick Duncombe had died the day before from meningitis.

Jason Leonard won his 100th cap in a hard-fought 25-17 victory, Jason Robinson scoring the England try after a break and sublime pass from Will Greenwood. Jonny Wilkinson's deadly boot providing the other 20 points, which took him past 600 in Test rugby.

Next it was the Millennium Stadium and a 26-9 victory over Wales. Greenwood scored England's first try and Joe Worsley crashed over less than a minute after replacing Neil Back. Wilkinson contributed another 16 points.

It was back to headquarters for Italy, who were beaten 40-5. England scored five tries in »

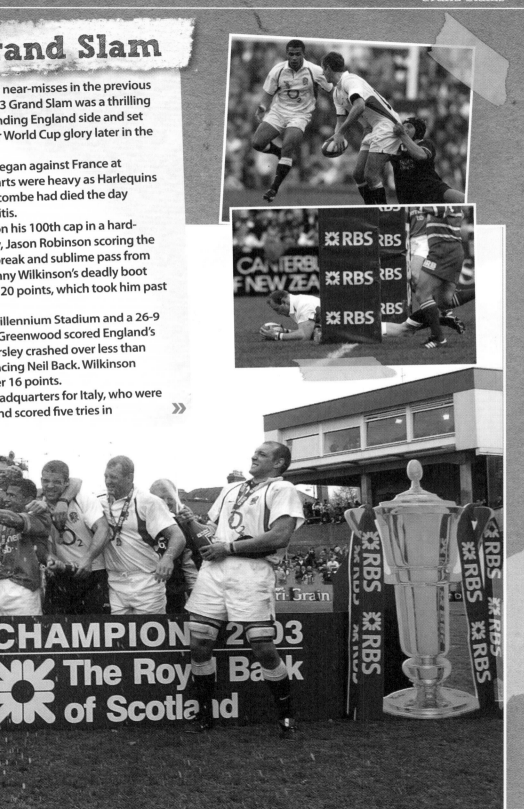

➤➤ the first 22 minutes. Josh Lewsey touched down first, followed by Steve Thompson, James Simpson-Daniel, then Lewsey again before Mike Tindall went over.

It was threatening to be a record-breaking rout but Italy managed to stem the flow and there was to be only one more try for England, as Dan Luger scored in the second half.

On the fourth weekend, Scotland were on the wrong end of a similar scoreline, 40-9. Lewsey got the only try of the first half before, in the second period, Ben Cohen grabbed a loose ball and went over. Two more tries from the dazzling Robinson sealed the win and another Grand Slam decider

awaited, this time against Ireland in Dublin.

In a crackling atmosphere, the home nation scored first through a David Humphreys drop-goal, but Lawrence Dallagio swiftly went over under the posts to send England on their way.

At 13-6 to England, the match was still in the balance approaching the hour mark when Tindall raced over for a decisive score. Five minutes later, Greenwood extended the lead with a third try for Clive Woodward's side. The centre went over again in the last 10 minutes before Dan Luger's try at the death capped a memorable day for English rugby, as Martin Johnson lifted the RBS 6 Nations trophy.

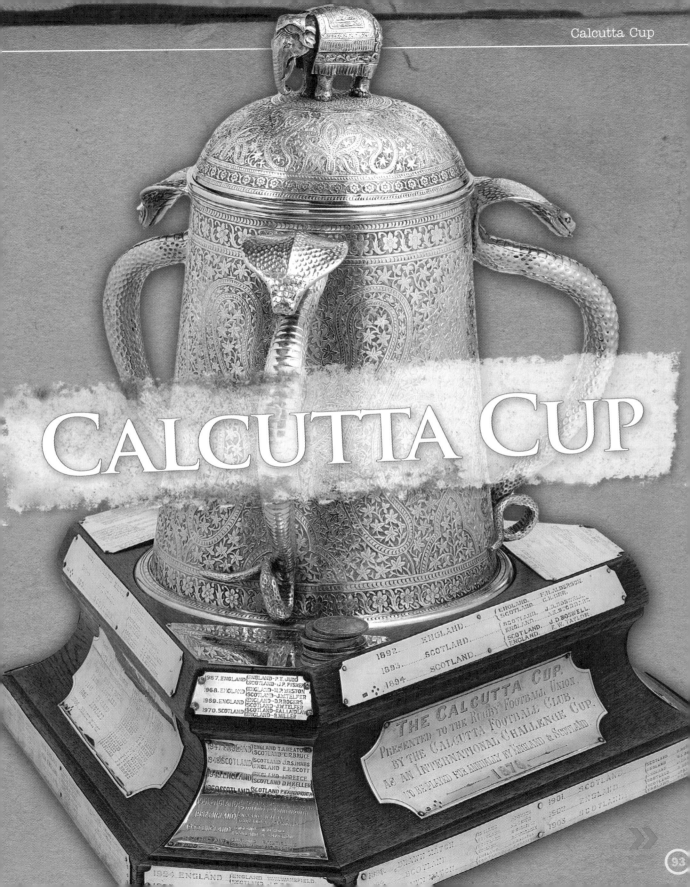

# CALCUTTA CUP

THE CALCUTTA CUP.
PRESENTED TO THE RUGBY FOOTBALL UNION,
BY THE CALCUTTA FOOTBALL CLUB,
AS AN INTERNATIONAL CHALLENGE CUP,
TO BE PLAYED FOR ANNUALLY BY ENGLAND & SCOTLAND.
1878.

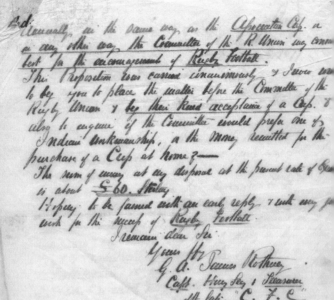

The original letters documenting the formation of the Calcutta Cup and, *below*, a portrait of England taking on Scotland in 1872

ENGLAND *versus* SCOTLAND

# The story of the Calcutta Cup

England versus Scotland is the oldest international football fixture in the world. When the contest was first played on March 27, 1871, the idea of two countries facing each other was a revelation and a revolution.

The instant appeal of the idea immediately ensured its longevity, especially because from 1879 onwards, the victors have played for The Calcutta Cup.

But how did a contest taking place in either Edinburgh or London become linked to an Indian city 5,000 miles away?

The answer lies in the Calcutta Football Club which was forced to close in 1878.

In January 1873, the popularity and impact of rugby in India had led to the

ENGLAND 9
SCOTLAND 3

MITSUBISHI ELECTRIC

## Now screening at Twickenham

**Although once strictly amateur on the field, rugby adopted some professional expertise in selling the game to the public. In 1983, two giant video screens were installed at Twickenham. Former England lock Peter Yarranton is seen here rehearsing his speech ahead of the Calcutta Cup match, when the screens were introduced.**

**The Calcutta Cup was damaged during a post-match incident following England's visit to Murrayfield in 1988**

formation of the club, which eventually joined the Rugby Football Union a year later.

However, the rising popularity of tennis and polo, plus the demands of running the British Empire, meant that playing numbers soon dwindled and the club was forced to close down.

Yet before the doors were shut forever, the club's committee decided that their memory should live on – and chose a very unique method to ensure this happened.

They raided what was left of the club's funds from the bank – 270 silver rupee coins to-the-then value of £60 – and had them melted down and forged into The Calcutta Cup.

The trophy is approximately 45cm high with three ornate cobra handles and an elephant on the lid, making it rugby's most ornate trophy.

The inscription on the wooden base reads: *"The Calcutta Cup presented to the Rugby Football Union by The Calcutta Football Club as an international challenge cup to be played for annually by England and Scotland 1878."*

The trophy had initially been earmarked for use as a club competition trophy but the RFU decided instead that it should be used for international competition.

At that time, England versus Scotland was the most popular fixture and it therefore seemed the perfect fit for the perfect piece of silverware. The Calcutta Cup was born.

## MY
# ENGLAND
## WILL CARLING

"England versus Scotland is the oldest rugby international. It oozes history, stories, experiences and emotion and that is why I love it. It is special – very, very special. And the history between England and Scotland does play a huge part in that, a vital part in that, and when I say history, I mean History!"

"I MADE MY ENGLAND DEBUT AGAINST SCOTLAND IN THE SIX NATIONS SO IT HOLDS A LOT OF SPECIAL MEMORIES FOR ME. IT'S A COMPETITION STEEPED IN TRADITION. YOU CAN SEE IT MEANS A LOT TO AN AWFUL LOT OF PEOPLE."

## MY
# ENGLAND
## BRAD BARRITT

"IT IS ALWAYS A MASSIVE OCCASION. YOU DON'T GET MANY OPPORTUNITIES TO PLAY SPECIAL GAMES LIKE THAT. BOTH SIDES WILL BE FULLY AWARE OF WHAT THE GAME MEANS AND THE HISTORY AND RIVALRY BETWEEN THE TWO COUNTRIES."

MY **ENGLAND**
CHRIS ROBSHAW

MY **ENGLAND**
JOSH LEWSEY

"The Calcutta Cup was so important to me. I loved playing at Murrayfield because I love the challenge and the pressure of trying to deliver there. The fixture has so much history and the hostile crowd was great. I loved the hostility and the more of that, the better. Playing at Murrayfield in a night game, where they've got 300 'Bravehearts' and pipers and everything else, for me that is where the chest goes out a little bit and you say 'right, bring it on boys'. Winning up there was always great. The Six Nations is a pilgrimage to me because you have all the history of the Celts versus the Anglo-Saxons. My mother is a history teacher so that was rammed down my throat as a child so I loved the challenge of it all."

# 2013 CALCUTTA CUP

England claimed their 66th Calcutta Cup victory, in the 120th edition of the match, with a comprehensive display at Twickenham.

Sean Maitland's early try for the visitors gave them brief hope of a first win in London since 1983 but England soon hit back and ended as dominant winners.

Chris Ashton, Billy Twelvetrees, Geoff Parling and Danny Care all scored tries while Owen Farrell contributed 18 points courtesy of four penalties and three conversions.

A late Stuart Hogg try and eight points from Greig Laidlaw meant the final score ended 38-18.

## Dream debut for Billy

In the long history of international rugby union, only a dozen Englishmen can boast that their first appearance for their country involved a try-scoring victory against Scotland.

The last man on that list is Billy Twelvetrees, who managed the feat as England retained the Calcutta Cup in the 2013 Six Nations.

He became the first man to start his England journey in such sensational style since Geoffrey Davies helped England to a narrow 23-17 win in the same fixture at Twickenham back in 1981.

Three decades may have passed but the excitement, nerves and anticipation felt by Davies remain exactly the same for every Calcutta Cup competitor, although the modern professional player works hard at harnessing the emotions surrounding the world's oldest international fixture.

"There was a lot of controlled excitement," Twelvetrees said. "Everyone was cool, calm and collected. Everybody knew the job we needed to do."

But what about the special feelings generated by a full house at Twickenham, and a full house hoping to open a Six Nations campaign with a victory?

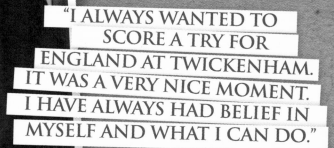

"I ALWAYS WANTED TO SCORE A TRY FOR ENGLAND AT TWICKENHAM. IT WAS A VERY NICE MOMENT. I HAVE ALWAYS HAD BELIEF IN MYSELF AND WHAT I CAN DO."

- Billy Twelvetrees

"You've just got to control your emotions," Twelvetrees added. "Obviously you get a bit worked up running out onto the pitch and during the anthems because it means a lot to you individually, but the senior players said to relax and try to enjoy myself. They told me it would be just like playing a big game for my club.

"I honestly felt quite relaxed – through the preparation in the week leading up to the game and even during it."

Twelvetrees immediately looked at home in the England midfield and pounced when the opportunity to score presented itself.

England had an eight-point lead going into the second half but Scotland were by no means out of the contest. Just two minutes after the interval, Twelvetrees seized his moment and crashed over the try-line from close range to give England some breathing space. They never looked back, eventually winning by a comfortable 20-point margin.

"My initial emotion was relief more than anything to get over the line and give the team a good start to the second half," Twelvetrees said.

"But as I ran back, I felt ecstatic and thought 'Blimey, I've just scored a try on my England debut at Twickenham. That's pretty cool'."

Indeed it was "pretty cool" – but not as cool as getting back to the changing rooms after the match and celebrating the victory with the rest of the England players and backroom staff.

"I looked around at the all boys, and at the Calcutta Cup in front of me," he remembered. "I thought to myself 'what an honour this is'."

## Royal approval

Twickenham has always had Royal approval as rugby enthusiast King George V was present for the stadium's first international against Wales in 1910.

The King was a frequent visitor to the ground and was always keen to praise England's victories, as his letter following their 1923 Grand Slam shows.

*England & Wales. January 1910.*

*...mon Kilner    H.R.H The Prince of Wales. (Now King George V.)*

The Daily Mirror, Monday, February 16, 1914.

# Wife Fights with Masked Robbers and Puts Them to Flight: Pictures.

# The Daily Mirror

LATEST CERTIFIED CIRCULATION MORE THAN 800,000 COPIES PER DAY.    One Halfpenny.

No. 3,218.    Registered at the G.P.O. as a Newspaper.    MONDAY, FEBRUARY 16, 1914

## THE KING AT THE RUGBY INTERNATIONAL.    MR. C. E. F...

*The King's smiling greeting to Mr. Asquith on arriving on the ground.*

*The King keenly following the game. Seated next to him is the Premier.*

WINDSOR CASTLE.    3rd. April, 1923.

Private.

My dear Davies,

The King wishes me to let you know how delighted he was to hear of the victory of the English team in Paris, and to congratulate you on being Captain of the winning team in all four matches.

His Majesty feels sure that you must have created a record by this most fitting termination to your brilliant career in International Football.

Yours sincerely,

Clive Wigram

Constructor Lieut Commander
W.J.A. Davies, O.B.E.
The Dockyard,
Portsmouth.

Two portraits of Mr. Charles Edward Fenner, the missing London ... through whom Lord Murray of Elibank purchased ... taken by the police in Paris

England v Wales
0
England v Ireland
15
England v Scotland
3

January 18th 1913.

ICH DIEN

ENGLAND
1913
IRELAND

England
v.
New Zealand
1925.

England
v. Wales

## Touch of brilliance

Modern day touch flags lack the colour, drama and intricacy of those from a bygone era.

Touch flags tend to have a generic look to them with the relevant tournament's name attached as well as the name of a major sponsor splashed all over them.

However, as these examples show, that was not always the case.

Once upon a time, touch flags were a true work of art.

Many hundreds of hours of skill and care were taken as cotton was delicately embroidered on to expensive silk flags, ensuring a lifelong memento of the occasion for anyone fortunate enough to get one once the game was complete.

# The Hillary Shield

When Sir Edmund Hillary, the first man to conquer Mount Everest, died in January 2008, tributes poured in from around the world.

Campaigns were launched to rename mountains in his honour and the Queen also attended a thanksgiving service for the famed New Zealander to pay tribute to his extraordinary achievement.

The rugby world also moved swiftly to show its own respects to Hillary who, along with Tenzig Norgay, finally made it to the top of the world on May 29, 1953.

Shortly after his death, it was announced that the Hillary Shield would be presented to the winning team following future Test matches between England and New Zealand.

Hillary's widow, Lady June Hillary, said at the time: "Ed was a real rugby fan who was always enthusiastic about the game and the All Blacks.

"He really enjoyed his rugby when he had the time to watch it, so I am very pleased that his name will be linked to New Zealand and England in this way."

Legendary All Blacks captain Richie McCaw also felt that the trophy would add new meaning and desire to one of rugby's oldest and most intriguing international fixtures.

He said: "Sir Ed put New Zealand on the map through his expeditions and also through what he achieved elsewhere. He was also a humble sort of character despite the great things he had accomplished.

## MY ENGLAND
### RICHARD COCKERILL

"I believe that I did the right thing that day. They were throwing down a challenge and I showed them I was ready to accept it. I'm sure they would rather we did that than walk away.

It was my first start in a Test match and I was obviously quite excitable. I thought 'I'm going to find Norm [Hewitt, the New Zealand hooker] stand opposite him' and I thought 'come on mate, let's have a go.'"

"They are attributes that you like to see in people and are attributes that the All Blacks aspire to."

The nine kilogram trophy, which measures over two feet in diameter, was comfortably won by New Zealand in the first three years of its existence as they ran riot at Twickenham.

It took England until December 1, 2012, to finally break their losing streak as captain Chris Robshaw finally got his hands on the trophy following England's 38-21 victory.

## Head honchos

It was the tradition for Springbok teams to award such a head to the first non-international team to beat them on a tour. This head was won by the London Counties team in 1951 when they played their match against the Springboks at Twickenham.

## Twickenham discovery

During work to improve the drainage of the pitch at Twickenham, this horse shoe was uncovered under the soil. Different theories exist on its origins. It could have come from one of the horses who pulled the heavy lawn mowers used by the Twickenham groundsmen or it may also be from one of the horses that were allowed to graze on the pitch during the First World War when rugby matches were suspended.

RFU

## Tough game to call

This telephone was presented to the RFU by Wales and The Marches Telecom Board when Wales faced England in February 1983. The game, played at Cardiff Arms Park as a Five Nations encounter, ended 13-13.

## Instrumental tour

The RFU were presented with this didgeridoo during their tour to Australia in 1979. It was a gift from their hosts, the Dubbo Rugby Union.

## Gift from the East

This ornamental trophy was presented to the RFU by the Toshiba Rugby Football Club 1984.

# VAULT

**From Springbok heads to salt and pepper pots, the Twickenham World Rugby Musuem has some weird and wonderful items in its treasure trove. Here are just a selection of the interesting exhibits displayed at the home of rugby...**

## From Russia with love

This carved wooden bear was a gift from the Russian Rugby Union to the England XV team on the occasion of their game on September 7, 1991. The game was played at Twickenham and the England XV won 53–0. The Russia National Rugby Union team is nicknamed the 'Bears'. The date on this Russian gift indicates that it was produced just over three months before the disbandment of the Soviet Union on December 26, 1991. The bear and base appear to have been carved from one piece of wood and is styled in a traditional pose. It is possible that it was made in Bogorodsk, now known as Noginsk, an old town near Moscow. Acclaimed for its master wood carvers since the 16th century, the village was once known as Medvezhy Ugol, which translates into 'Bear's Corner' or 'Bear Place' because of the thick woods surrounding it. When the players returned to their country following the 1991 tour they discovered the Soviet Union had been dissolved.

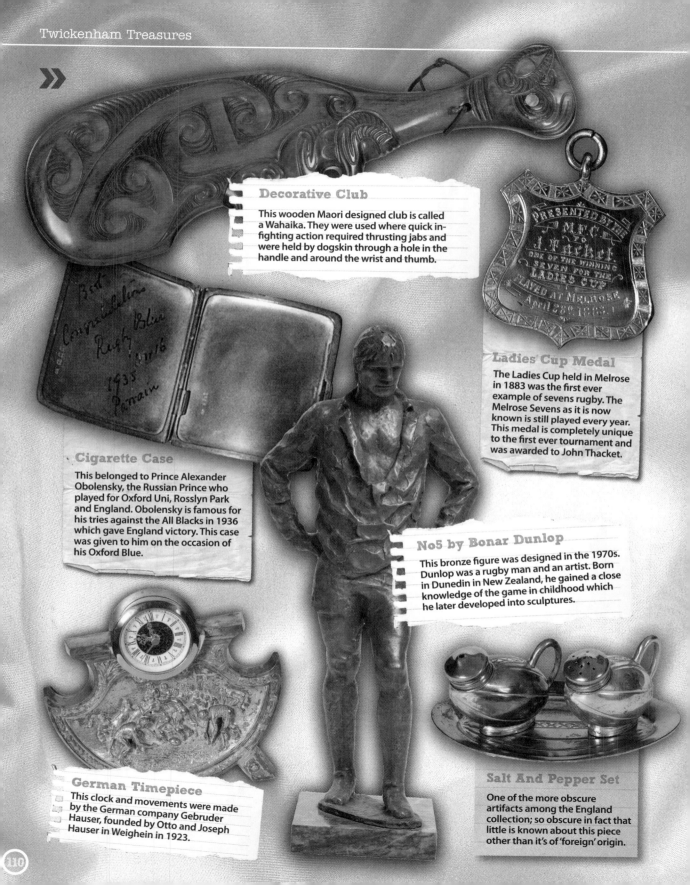

## Decorative Club

This wooden Maori designed club is called a Wahaika. They were used where quick in-fighting action required thrusting jabs and were held by dogskin through a hole in the handle and around the wrist and thumb.

## Ladies' Cup Medal

The Ladies Cup held in Melrose in 1883 was the first ever example of sevens rugby. The Melrose Sevens as it is now known is still played every year. This medal is completely unique to the first ever tournament and was awarded to John Thacket.

## Cigarette Case

This belonged to Prince Alexander Obolensky, the Russian Prince who played for Oxford Uni, Rosslyn Park and England. Obolensky is famous for his tries against the All Blacks in 1936 which gave England victory. This case was given to him on the occasion of his Oxford Blue.

## No5 by Bonar Dunlop

This bronze figure was designed in the 1970s. Dunlop was a rugby man and an artist. Born in Dunedin in New Zealand, he gained a close knowledge of the game in childhood which he later developed into sculptures.

## German Timepiece

This clock and movements were made by the German company Gebruder Hauser, founded by Otto and Joseph Hauser in Weighein in 1923.

## Salt And Pepper Set

One of the more obscure artifacts among the England collection; so obscure in fact that little is known about this piece other than it's of 'foreign' origin.

GRAND HOLIDAY ATTRACTION!
## RUGBY FOOTBALL MATCH
## WALES V. ENGLAND
ON THE
## FOOTBALL GROUND
ANSTEY,
EASTER MONDAY MORNING, April 24th
KICK-OFF 11 A.M.

## CARDIFF JUNIORS
V.
## LEICESTER JUNIORS

COME IN CROWDS!
ADMISSION, 3d.  BOYS, 2d.  ALL

### Advertising Poster

Made in 1905 by W.Wheelhouse, this poster advertised a game between England and Wales. Before Twickenham was England's home, international matches were played all over the country.

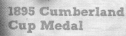

### 1895 Cumberland Cup Medal

This was presented to Edward Flynn (b. 1870 d. 1945) who played for Seaton RC in the 1890s. He helped the side win the Cumberland Cup in 1895.

### Bob Hiller Rosette

Bob Hiller won 19 caps for England between 1968 and 1972, playing seven of these games as captain. He was also a Baa Baa and took part in two Lions tours, in 1968 and 1971.

BOB HILLER

ENGLAND

### Kemp's RFU Blazer

RFU blazer dating from 1937. This was worn by D.T. Kemp. Kemp was one of the few international players to span WWII. He won five caps between 1937-1948 and was president of the RFU in 1971/72.

### Football Stout

Made by Duckworth and Co. (Essence) Ltd. Manchester. The company was founded in 1885 by William Duckworth and remained in family ownership for 118 years until they sold it to Cargill in 2003.

FOOTBALL STOUT

A SPLENDID WINTER DRINK

## Heading Down Under
This early cap comes from the 1888 Anglo-Australian Tour.

## Knight of the realm
1919-20 cap belonging to former England captain Wavell Wakefield, who later became a Conservative MP as well as serving as President of the RFU. The flanker's international debut came in a 19-5 defeat to Wales in Swansea. He was knighted in 1944.

## Losing start
1933 England cap belonging to Tony Roncoroni, whose first appearance came against Wales in a 7-3 Home Nations defeat at Twickenham.

The awarding of caps in rugby is a tradition that stems from Rugby School itself.

Rugby's School House team of 1839 was the first side to adopt a uniform. All their players wore red velvet caps with gold tassels during a match attended by the Dowager, Queen Adelaide. This is the first recorded occasion of a uniform being worn in a match.

The practice of cap wearing continued into the 1840s, so that fellow team players could be identified.

The school cap developed into the tradition of presenting a player with an honour cap. It continued as the international game became established and 'caps' were awarded when a player first represented his country. Occasionally they were awarded as players entered the field of play.

It is now an established term of reference for a player's appearance for a national team across a range of sports. Actual caps are not necessarily awarded for each individual appearance but, metaphorically, it is said that a player reaching 100 international appearances will "have won 100 caps".

## Stoop-erstar

Cap belonging to former England captain Adrian Stoop and, as the inside shows, manufactured by Veasey & Son. Stoop's debut came in an 8-0 defeat to Scotland during the 1905 Home Nations encounter at Richmond.

## Sixties cap

This England cap was issued between 1960-67.

## First edition

This programme is from England's first-ever international at Twickenham in 1910. Adrian Stoop's side beat Wales 11-6 in front of 18,000 spectators This single sheet, priced one penny, contained the match basics, such as the team line-ups and the programme of music.

## Commercial interest

Advertisers soon realised that getting their product on to the England programme could help boost sales.

## Going green

England drew 6-6 with Ireland at Twickenham in their 1925 Five Nations encounter. The matchday programme had changed little in 15 years, although this one demonstrates some appropriate use of green print.

1910 programme: ENGLAND v WALES, SATURDAY, JAN. 15th, 1910. Kick-off 2.45 p.m.

1925 programme: OFFICIAL PROGRAMME — COLE COURT HOTEL, TWICKENHAM — ENGLAND v. IRELAND, Saturday, February 14th, 1925. Kick-off 3 p.m.

# Get with the programme

As with the sport itself, rugby matchday programmes are now unrecognisable from the early days of the game.

Programmes were designed to give snippets of team news as well as provide a boost to the RFU's coffers via advertising.

The early programmes were just a single sheet of paper containing the names of both teams plus the match date, but they quickly advanced to provide plenty of pre-match reading material.

In fact, the modern supporter would now feel lost without the plentiful player and team features, captain's notes and messages and detailed information on England's opponents.

The evolution of the programme has not finished with today's glossy publications either.

The RFU launched an interactive version of its matchday programme as an 'app' in March 2013.

This gives subscribers the opportunity to watch videos from within the England camp and also read the thoughts of various leading rugby writers.

It marks an exciting development in a matchday ritual that has always been evolving.

ENGLAND v. NEW ZEALAND
SATURDAY, 4th JANUARY, 1936
**PRICE TWOPENCE**

## Got it covered

As the matchday programme entered the 1930s, it became more familiar with the current day format. The advancement of the printing industry allowed for cover pictures and inside pages.

RUGBY FOOTBALL UNION

England

versus

President's Overseas XV

1871    1971

TWICKENHAM
SATURDAY 17th APRIL 1971

OFFICIAL PROGRAMME 10p.

---

RUGBY FOOTBALL UNION

ENGLAND
v
FRANCE

TWICKENHAM
SATURDAY 28th FEBRUARY
1953
ONE SHILLING

---

RUGBY FOOTBALL UNION

ENGLAND
v
WALES

TWICKENHAM
SATURDAY 6th MARCH
1982
Official Programme
Forty Pence

Secretary R.F.U.

---

## Taking on the world

These England matchday programmes span a 30-year period, from the early 1950s to the early '80s, and take in opposition from several continents. Among them is a President's Overseas XV – a team assembled from the most formidable foreign talent, including players from France, South Africa, Fiji, Australia and New Zealand. The match, arranged to celebrate the centenary of the RFU, was won by the President's Overseas XV, 28-11.

---

RUGBY FOOTBALL UNION

An
England
XV
v

U.S.A.

TWICKENHAM
SATURDAY, 15th OCTOBER
1977
OFFICIAL PROGRAMME
TWENTY PENCE

SECRETARY R.F.U.

---

RUGBY FOOTBALL UNION

ENGLAND
v
SOUTH
AFRICA

TWICKENHAM
SATURDAY 20th DECEMBER
1969
OFFICIAL PROGRAMME
ONE SHILLING AND SIXPENCE

R.F.U.

---

RUGBY FOOTBALL UNION

ENGLAND
v
AUSTRALIA

TWICKENHAM
SATURDAY 3rd NOVEMBER
1984
Official Programme
Fifty Pence

Secretary R.F.U.

THE SAVE & PROSPER INTERNATIONAL

## RUGBY FOOTBALL UNION

# ENGLAND
v
# SCOTLAND

TWICKENHAM
16th FEBRUARY 1991

SAVE &
PROSPER
THE INVESTMENT HOUSE

Secretary R.F.U.

Official Programme
(including 20p contribution to the Wavell Wakefield Youth Trust)

## Modern approach

Matchday programmes have become increasingly popular over the last two decades and the modern-day publications are glossy and packed with information.

They bring readers closer to the team than ever with exclusive interviews and detailed insight into what goes on behind the scenes.

A precious keepsake for many collectors, they continue to play a part in a fans' matchday experience, although the boom in digital technology means it is now accessible in other formats and not just print.

TWICKENHAM
THE HOME OF ENGLAND RUGBY

ENGLAND V FRANCE

The RBS 6 Nations Championship

OFFICIAL
PROGRAMME
£3.00
(including contribution to the
Wavell Wakefield Youth Trust)

SAVE &
PROSPER
THE INVESTMENT HOUSE

THE SAVE & PROSPER
INTERNATIONAL

# ENGLAND
v
# FRANCE

TWICKENHAM
1st MARCH 1997

KICK OFF ~ 3.00pm

INVESTEC CHALLENGE SERIES

## ENGLAND
v ARGENTINA

TWICKENHAM
STADIUM
SATURDAY 14th NOVEMBER 2009
KICK OFF 2.30PM
OFFICIAL PROGRAMME £5.00

Investec
Challenge Series

RUGBY FOOTBALL UNION

# ENGLAND
v
# IRELAND

THE SAVE & PROSPER INTERNATIONAL

THE 100th MATCH

TWICKENHAM
SATURDAY 19th MARCH 1988

OFFICIAL
PROGRAMME
£1·00
(Including 20p
contribution to
Charitable Trust)

SAVE &
PROSPER
THE INVESTMENT HOUSE

Secretary R.F.U.

THE SAVE & PROSPER INTERNATIONAL

# 2003: Feeling on top of the world

England arrived Down Under for the 2003 Rugby World Cup believing that they were the best side in the world.

By the time they flew home a month later with the William Webb Ellis Trophy safely aboard the plane, that optimism had been gloriously confirmed as Jonny Wilkinson's extra-time drop-goal helped Sir Clive Woodward's side edge past the tournament hosts 20-17.

It was the most amazing finish imaginable in the finest final the Rugby World Cup has witnessed.

England arrived in Australia as favourites and that expectation brought its own pressures and almost derailed Woodward's plans.

They opened their World Cup campaign with a blitzing victory over Georgia before underlining their strength in a 25-6 win against South Africa.

Samoa then gave England a huge scare in front of 50,000 in Melbourne but they managed to progress to the knockout stages.

A 111-13 destruction of Uruguay was next up and was an emphatic response to the Samoa game before England misfired again in their quarter-final showdown with Wales in Brisbane.

Martin Johnson's 2003
World Cup tracksuit

The final scoreline of 28-17 in England's favour does little to describe the scare Wales gave an England side that had lost the fluency and flair it had shown for the previous two years.

But no matter. Winning was winning.

In the rain-ruined semi-final against France, Wilkinson kicked England to a 24-7 victory courtesy of five penalties and three drop-goals.

That set up a return of the 1991 World Cup final which Australia had won 12-6. This time, however, the end result would be different.

A sensationally unpredictable game saw Australia take an early lead but a fantastic Jason Robinson try and some calm kicking from Wilkinson gave England a 14-9 half-time lead.

A breathless second half saw Elton Flatley keep Australia in touching distance of England with three penalties which saw the match finish at 14-14.

Extra-time brought more excitement and unbearable tension as England regained the lead thanks to a Wilkinson penalty before the nerveless Flatley kicked his own.

It appeared that a sudden death shoot-out would be required but in the 100th and final minute of the match, England forced one last line-out... they manoeuvred Wilkinson into range... and his right boot sealed England's magnificent victory.

## MY ENGLAND
### JASON ROBINSON

"You're always looking for opportunities and you know that in a World Cup final there will not be many so when the opportunity comes, you've got to strike – it's as simple as that.

I remember Lawrence breaking off and getting that half break, then the inside pass to Wilkinson, and when you look on the video, Ben Cohen was free on the inside of Jonny so he would have been straight under the post. Thankfully, because I was in Jonny's view, the pass came out to me and it was a case of 'ooomph, I'm going for it'. I pinned my ears back and went for the corner."

WORLD CUP FINAL TRY

# THE LINE-OUT

## MY ENGLAND
### BEN KAY

"We had worked on line-outs in training because Clive Woodward was convinced a big game would be won by a drop-goal – that shows his foresight – and that passage of play highlights everything we were about.

We were under the posts waiting for Elton Flatley to kick a penalty and Jonno said 'We'll kick off long and they will kick to touch. We're going to get a line-out, Benny what is the call?' We knew that Australia had worked hard at working out our line-out so it felt best to avoid the front and middle jumper and go to the back. They wouldn't be expecting that and I knew their main defence would be at the front.

I don't think Steve wanted to throw it because it's a much tougher throw, but he nailed it and Lewis Moody also deserves credit for taking the ball cleanly. He delivered a great ball, Mike Catt crashed the ball forward and the rest is history."

## MY ENGLAND
### LEWIS MOODY

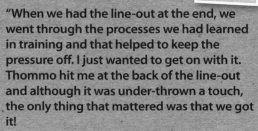

"When we had the line-out at the end, we went through the processes we had learned in training and that helped to keep the pressure off. I just wanted to get on with it. Thommo hit me at the back of the line-out and although it was under-thrown a touch, the only thing that mattered was that we got it!

We wanted Daws to be making the pass to Jonny so we had to recycle Matt out of the bottom of the ruck.

To allow that to happen, Backy hit Jonno with a short pass that let us recycle Daws out, he hit Jonny with the pass and he did the rest."

> "THAT KICK WASN'T STRAIGHT. I NEED TO KEEP WORKING."
>
> *Jonny Wilkinson*

"ONCE MATT DAWSON HAD MADE THE BREAK, FOLLOWED BY NEIL BACK, I TOOK IT UP ONCE MORE AND I THINK THERE WERE 30 SECONDS TO GO. WE THEN HAD WILKO IN FRONT OF THE STICKS TO WIN THE WORLD CUP AND YOU JUST WOULDN'T HAVE ANYONE ELSE THERE, WOULD YOU?"

## MY ENGLAND
### MARTIN JOHNSON

## MY ENGLAND
### JOSH LEWSEY

"Matt Dawson's little dart forward was so important as it changed Jonny's drop-goal chances from about 40% or 50% to 80%, even if it did mean our best passer was then at the bottom of a ruck. But then Jonno caught Neil Back's short pass to recycle the play again and get Matt back into the game and Jonny did the rest. That period of play summed up everything that was great about that World Cup team."

123

| | | Australia | England |
|---|---|---|---|
| 1 | Tries | 1 |
| 0 | Conversions | 0 |
| 4 | Penalties | 4 |
| 0 | Drop Goals | 1 |
| 17 | Score | 20 |

Extra Time

THE CELEBRATIONS

## MY ENGLAND
### MATT DAWSON

"To say we celebrated in style would be the understatement of the year. We've had a big one – an absolute blinder and I think it's been richly deserved. You can't underestimate the power of our supporters. The atmosphere all week was second to none."

## MY ENGLAND
### MARTIN JOHNSON

"It was a home game for Australia, albeit a World Cup final. They don't lose a lot of games in Sydney. For us to have – certainly where we were – parity in the stadium in terms of colours and fans was unbelievable. We weren't alone. We had a huge amount of support. It was a huge effort by the entire squad of players, coaches and backroom staff, everybody. "

## MY ENGLAND
### BEN KAY

"It's a good job you can't lip read because I shook the ref's hand at the end and I'm not sure how much I was thanking him! I then ran to the sidelines and we went mad. It was just relief really; relief that we had done it. When you get into the changing room, lock the doors and celebrate with all the people who had been on the journey with you, that is a very special moment. "

## MY ENGLAND
### JONNY WILKINSON

"We're overwhelmed. It matters so much to get this support and being on this bus now is one of the greatest moments of my life. It's great to be able to pay back the fans who travelled half way around the world as well as those who stayed at home."

# World BEATER

With an international career spanning 12 years, Lawrence Dallaglio has plenty of precious memories to draw upon, but there's one recollection that stands out above all others, an occasion etched into English sporting history...

A decade after the event, Lawrence Dallaglio's memories of his finest moment in an England shirt remain as fresh and as grin-provoking as ever.

Dallaglio was the only member of the England squad to play every single minute of the 2003 Rugby World Cup.

Nobody gave more for the cause. Nobody deserved more praise. Nobody derives more pleasure from those cherished moments.

Dallaglio and Co wrestled the William Webb Ellis Trophy out of the hands of the Southern Hemisphere for the first time and gave English sports fans their happiest occasion since Dallaglio's footballing counterparts won the 1966 World Cup.

Dallaglio's eyes brighten and his obvious joy comes bubbling to the surface when he discusses the journey that England took under Clive Woodward at the time.

And, just as he was on the pitch, the Wasps and England legend is as straightforward and as honest as can be.

"We were the better team," he said, when discussing the final against tournament hosts, Australia.

"We knew it, they knew it and we had beat them six times previously home and away, but you still have to go out there and prove it.

"England and Australia have incredible rivalry and they did very well to make it such a tough game but, on reflection, the better side won, definitely. We were the number one side and it was fitting that we were able to do it.

"But all credit to Australia for the way they fought and they made it very tough for us."

The final against Australia has rightly gone down as one of the greatest rugby matches of all time.

It pitted England – the supposedly ice-cool world No.1s – against the pluckier and more earthy Australia, a side who had shocked the rugby world with their fantastic semi-final victory over Antipodean neighbours New Zealand.

And while Dallaglio is right in his assertion that England were the stronger side, factors such as those fade to nothing when you're in the boiler room environment of a World Cup final.

"The games in the World Cup were closer than we would've liked, but that's what pressure does to you and what playing away from home does to you.

"Everyone plays their best game against England and lifts their game against the best team in the world so we knew it was going to be difficult."

# England World Cup Champions

What happened during the final in Sydney tested everybody; players, coaches and fans to the very limit.

"We should've been out of sight by half-time and Ben Kay might have made life easier for us!" Dallaglio grinned, remembering the 14-5 half-time score and the fact England's lead would have been much healthier if Kay had not knocked on when practically over the try-line just before the interval.

"The second half was a complete disaster but we kept thinking clearly. We were fit, we were strong, we had only used very few substitutes and that showed the strength and fitness we had.

"When the game went to extra-time, and at 17-17, we were focused, we didn't panic and we were ready.

"We were really super-fit and when you're super-fit, you are able to make the right decisions in the heat of battle at the right time. Clive used to call it T-Cup – 'thinking clearly under pressure'."

Forget teacups, England's fans back in the UK were reaching for the stronger stuff despite the early morning kick-off as nerves were stretched to breaking point.

However, when Jonny Wilkinson finally found his range and kicked the last-gasp drop-goal to win the match 20-17, the only drink required was Champagne, and it has never tasted better.

Dallaglio can easily recall the events leading up to Wilkinson's moment of brilliance.

He said: "Jonny had had a few goes at kicking a drop-goal in the final but when it mattered most, he nailed it.

"After Elton Flatley had levelled the scores at 17-all, we could've kicked off short to try and reclaim the ball but we didn't want to take a risk so we kicked long.

"We felt they wouldn't run it back and they would prefer to kick to touch to give us a line-out near the halfway line and that is what happened.

"The line-outs had been a mess and we were winning each other's ball but we threw to the back to have the element of surprise.

"There was still a lot to do but Matt Dawson made his famous break which was clearly what was needed because although Jonny Wilkinson is a magician he couldn't manage it from that far away. Martin Johnson then took it up and that got Jonny in range, and he nailed it.

"After that, Australia kicked short to Trevor Woodman, he made a terrific catch, we did enough to secure the ball and then Mike Catt kicked it over the top of my head and that was it – the end."

As the ball cannoned into the crowd and referee Andre Watson blew his whistle, a tremendous odyssey for the England side was reaching its wonderful, glorious conclusion.

Clive Woodward had made it his life's work to deliver a team capable of winning the World Cup. That team had done exactly as he had wished.

It was now time to celebrate.

"It was a great, great feeling and it was great to share that with all the supporters," Dallaglio said.

"To win the World Cup in Australia against Australia was special and it was one of those amazing moments in life that professional sportspeople occasionally get the chance to experience.

"The greatest feeling was when we got back into the changing room after the several laps of honour and had a very private moment, just as a group.

"Not just the team that played, but the

entire squad, the backroom staff and the back-up staff, and there was a variety of emotions.

"Some sat there laughing, some crying and it was the shared sense of collective achievement and success.

"We were put on this planet to be together and it is great to achieve things on your own but I think its a lot more fun to achieve things together.

"That was the end of an epic journey and I think we knew at that moment that this England team would never play together again.

"Jonny Wilkinson didn't play for England again for another four years and guys like Martin Johnson and Jason Leonard retired, so that was a very special moment – being together with our medals around our necks, enjoying that together.

"For many of us, our lives changed from that day."

Dallaglio is spot on with that assessment.

England's players had arrived in Australia as men who were relatively unheralded, especially in comparison to the column inches and fame afforded to England's football team.

By the time they flew back on a plane rechristened 'Sweet Chariot' in their honour a month later, they had become superstars.

For a short time, England were greeted like they were The Beatles, albeit with fewer Mop Tops and more cauliflower ears.

When they returned, thousands greeted them at Heathrow airport at four in the morning and tens of thousands more poured onto the streets of London to celebrate as the entire squad toured the city on an open-top bus tour.

Dallaglio cannot help but smile when he recalls those heady days.

"We were ushered onto the plane and we were sat in business class," he said. "Clive and the coaches were sat in first class, of course! The press officer at the time asked me and Jason Leonard to take the trophy around the plane and we said 'yes, we would be thrilled to do that' and it ended up taking us three and a half hours!

"Every single supporter wanted to touch the cup and there was complete euphoria.

"We were in high spirits between Sydney and Singapore and one or two requests went out to the air stewardess to bring the drinks trolley up.

"From Singapore to London we got back into World Cup mode and there was a responsibility to ensure we were in good shape when we arrived.

"When we got back we were informed by the police that there were a lot of fans waiting and we thought 'whatever', but they opened the doors and there were thousands.

"We forced Jonny out through the doors as the sacrificial lamb to the lions and it was amazing.

"Poor old Jonny didn't quite realise what was happening. He was the star of the show but had no idea. When we got to our hotel he said to Clive 'I'm going to get a cab back to Heathrow and then catch a flight to Newcastle' and they tried to explain to him that that wasn't a good idea and that he maybe needed a car to get back to Newcastle!

"He was so humble and so modest that he hadn't thought about the impact of what he had done.

"They were great days and great memories and the parade around London was the chance for fans here to celebrate and feel part of it.

"What we must remember is that playing for England is about England – it's not about the players, it's about the country, and you want to do your best for the country, and when you are successful, you want everyone to share that.

"The parade was such a great occasion because it was a celebration for everyone.

"The World Cup happened such a long way from home and supporters were watching it in pubs at 6am with a beer and a cooked breakfast.

"Although we had some idea what was going on back home, we couldn't really grasp it and how much it was being followed back in the UK."

As was proven, Dallaglio need not have been worried. The satisfaction he felt at winning the World Cup was replicated millions of times over by households up and down the nation.

And the satisfaction he feels now, 10 years on, remains as exhilarating and as thrilling as that rainy night in Sydney.

A rainy night in Sydney when Jonny Wilkinson drop-kicked a ball. And a rainy night in Sydney when England conquered the world.

# DOING IT FOR THE
# SHIRT

Often muddied, sometimes bloodied, the white armour of England is stained with pride and passion. From its origins at Rugby School, the shirt - and the famous Red Rose emblem - has undergone a series of cosmetic changes over the years, but each adaptation has produced an army of heroes...

# History of the England kit

One virtually unchangeable aspect of English rugby has been the national side's kit and colours.

In fact, if you looked at an England jersey from the first international in 1872 and compared it to a modern shirt, then the similarities are huge.

Despite the tweaks to the design over the last two decades, England have always worn a predominantly white kit with a red rose over the left breast.

Various theories are put forward as to why England have always played in those colours but the likeliest explanation stems from Rugby School.

The school's emblem is a red rose and they also traditionally played in white kit so it is possible that this was adopted as the national side's colours as a reflection of the game's background.

Another potential reason is that the rose

## Full of Eastern promise

The shirt worn by the England XV on their tour of the Far East in 1971. The team played seven matches in the September and October, winning all seven.

FAR EAST TOUR 1971

## The outlook is rosy

This 1930s England jersey is one of the first examples of the shirt with a standardised rose. Before this, all the players had worn different stylised roses. The standardised rose was designed by Alfred Wright, an employee of the Rugby Football Union based at Twickenham. The design did not change until the late 1990s when it was updated as part of the redesign of the Union's corporate branding.

is the county symbol for Lancashire and was chosen because the RFU Board that picked England's first side contained two representatives from Lancashire clubs.

England's cotton kit did not change much at all from 1872 until 1992 when blue and red stripes and a red collar were introduced.

This opened the door to the more frequent changes we have seen since.

In fact there have been over 30 new England shirts used in the last 20 years as well as a complete revolution in the design and fabrics used.

Cotton Traders designed England's shirts until Nike took over in 1997 and they introduced the most radical change yet in the summer of 2003.

England were looking for that extra edge over their opponents so Nike created a tighter fitting shirt that was designed to cling to England's players and make them harder to tackle.

The lighter material also ensured better temperature control and gave England a

**»**

**Early knitwear**

A 1905 England Schoolboy jersey. This was worn during the second ever schoolboy international match, played against Wales, in 1905.

further advantage. The idea was instantly popular and has since been followed by every international side.

Nike were replaced by Canterbury as England's kit suppliers in 2012 and their "England Is All" ethos seeks to celebrate rugby from the grassroots right up to the national team.

They have advanced the kit further with the claim the modern-day England shirt cannot be ripped off by an opponent.

The high strength fibres help the shirt hug the modern player's physique like never before and the lightweight design also helps England's stars remain as cool as possible in the heat of battle.

England Sevens captain, Rob Vicerkman, said: "Winning is often about the smallest margins and the technology in the Canterbury shirt is right up there.

"With sevens now being an Olympic sport, every team is going to be looking for that extra crucial edge."

## MY ENGLAND
## LEWIS MOODY

"The new shirts were great because if you made a break, you knew you weren't going to be pulled back and also, psychologically, it was a big advantage because it made us feel like we were leading the way in every area. We were setting the examples and trying to be the best in the world in fitness, nutrition and training, and the shirts were another area where we felt we were excelling.

I'm not sure all the front row boys agreed because they were a bit tight, but we all felt they were very important. "

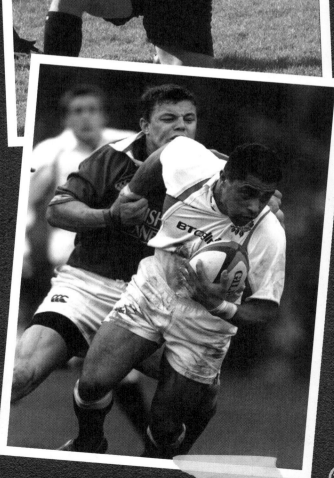

## MY ENGLAND
### LAWRENCE DALLAGLIO

"The history of the shirt has evolved over the years and England were always pretty traditional in the way we produced it. Certain sections of the RFU always felt it should just be white with a red rose, but the introduction of the tight-fitting shirt came from Clive Woodward.

England used to be a team that copied other people. We were followers. We looked at New Zealand and South Africa and a year later we copied it but by that time they had moved on. When we started beating them on a regular basis, we became the leaders and they were the followers.

Clive always felt that if England were going to win the World Cup, it would be a partnership, we couldn't do it on our own. So he got all our partners in the room and asked for help and told Nike that he wanted a new shirt designed for the World Cup because that could be the difference between wining and losing.

He told them that he had Jason Robinson, an amazing player who was as fast as lightning and he didn't want him grabbed by the shirt. Nike took that on board very quickly and they »

# MY ENGLAND
## CHRIS ROBSHAW

"The current Canterbury kit is nice and vibrant and it is pretty brilliant. I'm sure some of the guys will try and rip the collars – that is one of the tests they have to do.

The blue socks are back and they are a crowd favourite and one that everyone enjoys.

Everybody can be part of it and that's what it's all about, rugby being connected, and we have a reminder in the shirt that everything is connected and we should give back as much as possible. If we can inspire people too, all the better."

**Ben Clarke and Dean Richards**

## Kit fact

England's current Canterbury kit has 'England Connected' embroidered on the inside sleeve – an idea from Head Coach Stuart Lancaster – in a bid to inspire all England teams to remember their roots and remind them that they're representing the entire country.

» came back after a series of meetings with the tight-fitting shirt.

The backs had a more figure hugging design and the forwards would have liked a more figure hugging one, but it wasn't possible! It was one of the few areas where New Zealand and South Africa copied us. They might not admit it, but England pioneered that shirt. It was introduced against France in Marseilles. It was modelled by the then captain Dorian West and also Jason Leonard. They seemed to be going very red throughout the national anthem and remained red for the next hour and a half!!

It was an incredible innovation that came from Clive. You can't deny that he was a pioneer and innovator and he made sure no stone was left unturned in his pursuit to win England the World Cup. Of course, the players ultimately delivered, but the extra one per cent made the difference and that shirt definitely made the difference between scoring tries and not scoring tries.

I always feel that playing for England is very, very special. I don't think anyone has any right to play for England and the shirt is only lent to you for a period of time. It is your responsibility to honour that shirt and enhance it and go out and fill the shirt and then pass it on to the next player.

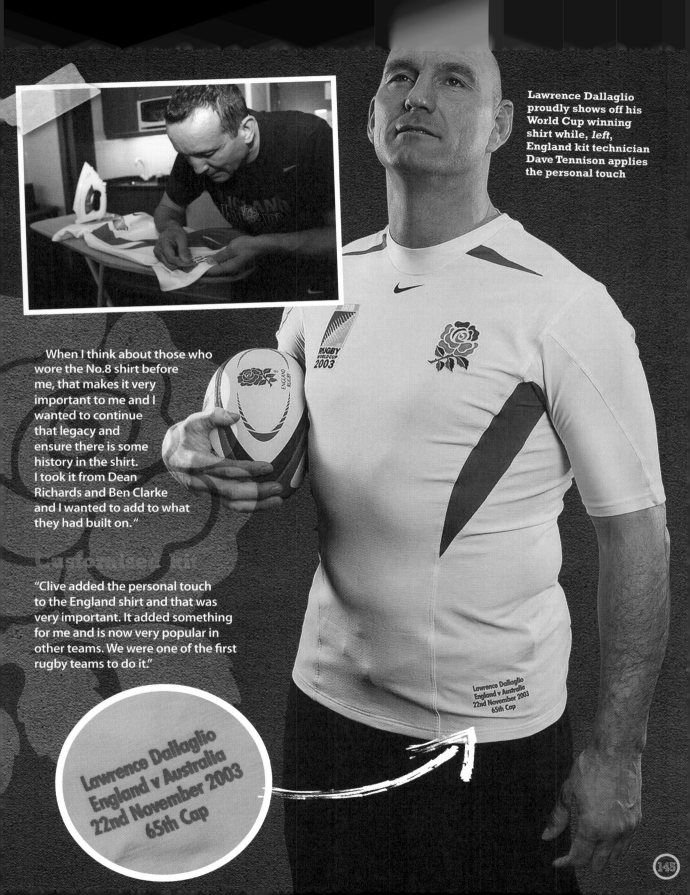

Lawrence Dallaglio proudly shows off his World Cup winning shirt while, *left*, England kit technician Dave Tennison applies the personal touch

When I think about those who wore the No.8 shirt before me, that makes it very important to me and I wanted to continue that legacy and ensure there is some history in the shirt. I took it from Dean Richards and Ben Clarke and I wanted to add to what they had built on. "

## Customised kit

"Clive added the personal touch to the England shirt and that was very important. It added something for me and is now very popular in other teams. We were one of the first rugby teams to do it."

Lawrence Dallaglio
England v Australia
22nd November 2003
65th Cap

Jason Robinson
England v South Africa
20th October 2007

# Painful memories

After a sensational seven years in rugby union, Jason Robinson brought the curtain down on his England career in the most painful way possible. A dislocated shoulder in the 2007 Rugby World Cup final was not the fitting end that Robinson deserved and his playing shirt had to be cut open so his damaged shoulder could be treated swiftly by England medics.

Although 'Billy Whizz' could not add a second World Cup winner's medal to his collection, he did leave the field to a standing ovation from England and South Africa fans alike as they recognised that a modern great was leaving the stage for the last time.

Robinson said: "It was a sad way to finish. I wanted to play the 80 minutes and try to make a difference, but it wasn't to be.

"I went in to secure the ball and a few of their guys came over and smashed me in contact. I knew my shoulder had gone. I knew it was over and the end of my game. I knew it was my last."

Toby Flood
England v South Africa
20th October 2007

## Flood barrier

Toby Flood's shirt from the 2007 Rugby World Cup final against South Africa. England lost 15-6 in the Stade de France, Paris.

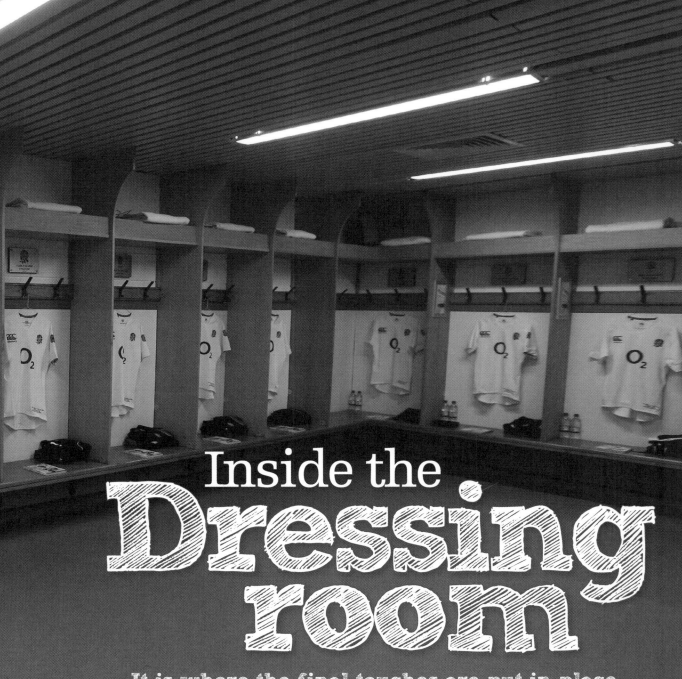

# Inside the
# Dressing room

It is where the final touches are put in place ahead of battle. It is the place where players perform rituals, rejoice and regroup.
It is England's sanctuary.

Will Greenwood was a familiar face in the Twickenham dressing room for many years

# MY ENGLAND
## WILL GREENWOOD

ENGLAND RUGBY

"The changing room has amazing fond memories; 82,000 people out there, but you can't hear a thing. It's like a tomb before the game.

That is when you see who you want on your team – you see it in their eyes – and, in the team I played in, every single one of them had it in the eyes.

Rugby is a contact sport and you have 80 minutes to get one over them, so you have to get yourself ready. Everybody has their own repetitive routines and, once you're in here, you don't change.

There are a few people slapping each

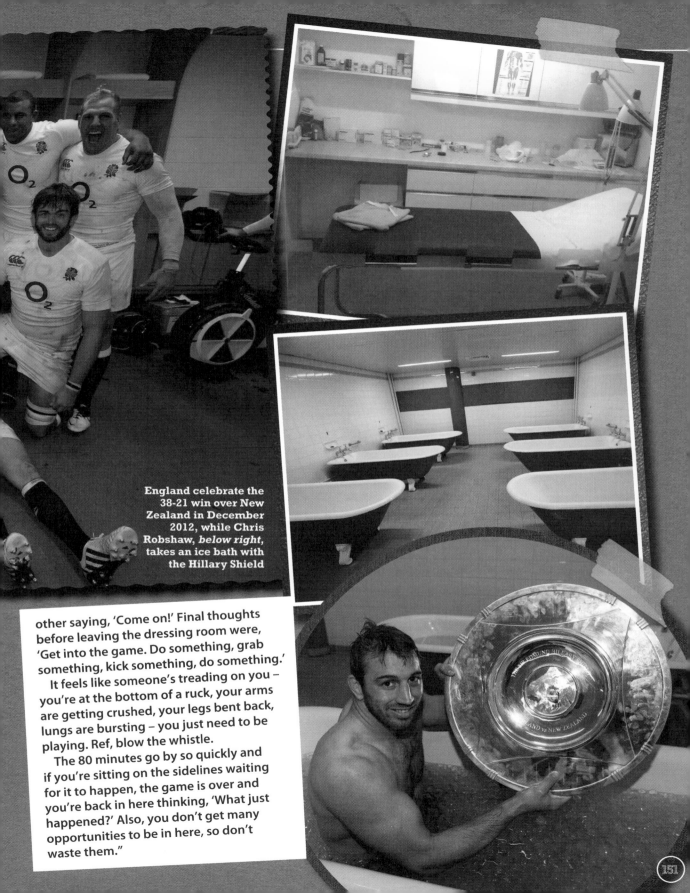

England celebrate the 38-21 win over New Zealand in December 2012, while Chris Robshaw, *below right*, takes an ice bath with the Hillary Shield

other saying, 'Come on!' Final thoughts before leaving the dressing room were, 'Get into the game. Do something, grab something, kick something, do something.'

It feels like someone's treading on you – you're at the bottom of a ruck, your arms are getting crushed, your legs bent back, lungs are bursting – you just need to be playing. Ref, blow the whistle.

The 80 minutes go by so quickly and if you're sitting on the sidelines waiting for it to happen, the game is over and you're back in here thinking, 'What just happened?' Also, you don't get many opportunities to be in here, so don't waste them."

"I sat in the same position in the changing room for my entire career, which was very nice.

I had a pre-match ritual of always taking a ball onto the pitch to bounce around. This helped me mentally prepare.

Dave Tennison (England Kit Manager) always used to leave a ball in my locker. All the others are normally in the bag, ready for Jonny (Wilkinson) or Floody (Toby Flood) or whoever to go out and kick, but he would always leave one in my locker. Those little things used to always help with your preparation; it was one last thing I didn't have to think about – that is the level of care and preparation that goes into a game."

**Work done by staff behind the scenes helps lead to success**

## MY ENGLAND
### LAWRENCE DALLAGLIO

"Bearing in mind I made my debut on the cusp of amateur and professional rugby, it's perfectly fair to say that if I was making my debut today my initiation could be somewhat different.

Traditions needed to be upheld but luckily I had my great mate Jason Leonard, who'd already earned nearly 50 caps by the time I made my first. That was a good thing... I think! He made sure I didn't have too many pre-match nerves and also made sure I couldn't feel any of my nerves after the game!

On the bus I sang an Italian operatic song but you get the first bar off and then everyone drowns you out and starts throwing things at you and abusing you generally!

It was a fun experience, my first cap. I came off the bench, replacing Tim Rodber, and we had a decent period and scored a try through Phil de Glanville. Although we lost, I came off the pitch and couldn't wipe the smile off my face because I had just made my debut while everyone else was sad and glum because we had lost to South Africa."

## MY ENGLAND
### BEN KAY

"I chose to sing 'Green Green Grass of Home' by Tom Jones. I still don't know why! I think it's because I knew the words. I did okay, I think there had been some particularly terrible ones before me so I didn't disgrace myself too much."

"As the new cap, I was asked to stand up and sing a song. God knows why I sang 'Help' by the Beatles – it's got a few nasty high notes and I don't exactly have a great voice. It may sound mad, but I was more nervous about singing than playing the game."

# Inside view of Twickenham

A Twickenham full house, ready and waiting for an England battle on a shimmering green pitch, is enough to take the breath away.

However, the stadium's attraction is not just consigned to what happens on the field.

The stadium manages to mix pageantry and prestige in equal measure and from the luxuries of the President's Suite to the custom of the after-match dinner, players old and new enjoy the history and tradition that comes as part of the Twickenham package.

RUGBEIA · FLOREAT · UBIQUE

## MY ENGLAND
### RFU President, Paul Murphy

### The President's Suite...

"The President's Suite at Twickenham is one of the most special places in rugby. The opportunity to dine at the Home of England Rugby beneath historic paintings with a view of the pitch is a special experience. No other rugby citadel has a room with the same unique and historic ambience.

The suite is presided over by the President of the Rugby Football Union. His Vice-Presidents host the other tables in the room. From royalty to heads of state to visiting unions, the experience and memories are long lasting."

### Post-match dinner...

"To be present at a post-match team dinner is to enjoy rugby heaven. These are formal events where guests, the two teams and match officials join together to eat and refresh themselves after the rigours of the day.

A look in any direction reveals a rugby celebrity. Formal speeches of welcome and congratulations are delivered by the opposing presidents before the respective captains exchange words of wisdom on the match performance and exchange gifts for their teams. The match officials contribution is always acknowledged, generally with a tie or two.

While the speeches are formal, the atmosphere is relaxed with players, coaches and officials all willing to engage in views on the match and what might have been…. A few autographs or a picture usually provide a lasting memory of a special rugby evening."

# ON THE
# BALL

The destiny of the oval game, particularly the matchball, has literally been reshaped since its early inception. From pig's bladder, leather-encased, hand-stitched compositions, to the modern-day synthetically engineered, rubber-lined prolate spheroid, it's evolution has brought about a whole new ball game...

RICHARD LINDON
1816-1887
INVENTOR

# A whole new ball game...

The modern rugby ball is very different from the early incarnations two centuries ago, which were created from an inflated pig's bladder.

William Gilbert opened a cobbler's in Rugby in the early 1800s and was soon supplying balls to Rugby School. These balls, which varied in shape and size, were encased in hand-stitched, four-panel leather casings to prevent them from bursting. They were an oval shape, larger and rounder than what is used today, and could be kicked a long distance.

Gilbert was renowned for inflating bladders by lung power, using a clay pipe stem which was inserted into the opening of the bladder. A rival ball maker, Richard Lindon, employed a similar technique, sadly with tragic consequences: Lindon's wife died after contracting a disease from blowing up pigs' bladders.

## Early balls not a 'round' for long

Early rugby balls were virtually round and varied in size because their shape depended on the pig bladder used inside. They eventually evolved to a standardised size following the invention of vulcanised rubber.

As a result, Lindon pioneered the use of rubber bladders following Charles Goodyear's invention of vulcanised rubber. This meant that the balls could be manufactured to a uniform size and regulated, which became an RFU stipulation in 1892.

The modern shape evolved to improve handling and passing, as these skills became more important than kicking.

It wasn't until the late 1970s that alternatives to leather were first used, as synthetic materials gradually became established.

A regulation ball is 28-30cm long, 58-62cm in circumference at its widest point and 74-77cm end to end. It may be treated to make it water resistant and easier to grip.

Gilbert remains the primary ball manufacturer in the sport, and will be the official ball supplier for the 2015 Rugby World Cup.

### Signed by Springboks

Ball signed by the British Isles teams of 1955 and 1962 and the 1955 South Africa side.

### SLAZENGER
MADE IN ENGLAND
### VICTORY

### Mighty All Blacks

Slazenger ball signed by the 1963-64 New Zealand team who were unbeaten on their tour of Britain and France, producing a 14-0 win at Twickenham on Jan 4, 1964.

### Mitre
OFFICIAL MATCH BALL
RUGBY WORLD CUP 1987
5

### Taking on the world

Mitre matchball from the very first Rugby World Cup, hosted by New Zealand in 1987. England's progress was halted by Wales at the quarter-final stage.

### Mitre BOK

### New kid on the Bok

South African Mitre Bok matchball with its distinctive orange and black writing.

### A worthy cause

Matchball from Northern Hemisphere v Southern Hemisphere Tsunami Aid Match held at Twickenham on March 5, 2005.

### EUROPEAN CHAMPIONSHIPS
NICE 2-6th April 1997
OPERATION BALLONS
### GILBERT
ENGLAND 24 — SCOTLAND 8    1823 SIZE 5
FFR

### Women's Euro delight

Matchball from 1997 Women's European Championships. England beat Scotland 24-8.

## Final heartache

A matchball from the 1991 World Cup final between England and eventual winners Australia.

**adidas**
Official Match Ball. Rugby World Cup.
1991

THE BRITISH LIONS
NATIONAL SPORTING CLUB SPORTING CLUB
25 TH OCT. 1971

MENU

Truite fumée
Sauce Raifort

Oxtail clair
au Xérès
Paillettes dorées

Carre d'Agneau
Persillé

Brocolis au Beurre
Pommes Parmentier

Salade de Fruits
rafraichis

Torta Zabaglione
semifreddo

Café

## Hungry Lions

This ball celebrates the British and Irish Lions' successful tour to New Zealand in 1971. Specially produced, it had a menu printed on it, presumably for a dining function for the players and staff.

GILBERT
PUMAS 96
SIZE 5

## Loss Pumas

Gilbert ball signed by the Argentina team in 1996, following their 20-18 defeat to England.

ENGLAND RUGBY

## Modern design

A more up-to-date Gilbert matchball signed by the England side.

GILBERT
MURRAYFIELD
SIZE

## Aussie offering

A Gilbert 'Murrayfield' ball signed by the 1988 Australian touring party.

GILBERT
BARBARIAN
official ENGLAND matchball

## England in the '90s

Official England matchball from 1998.

167

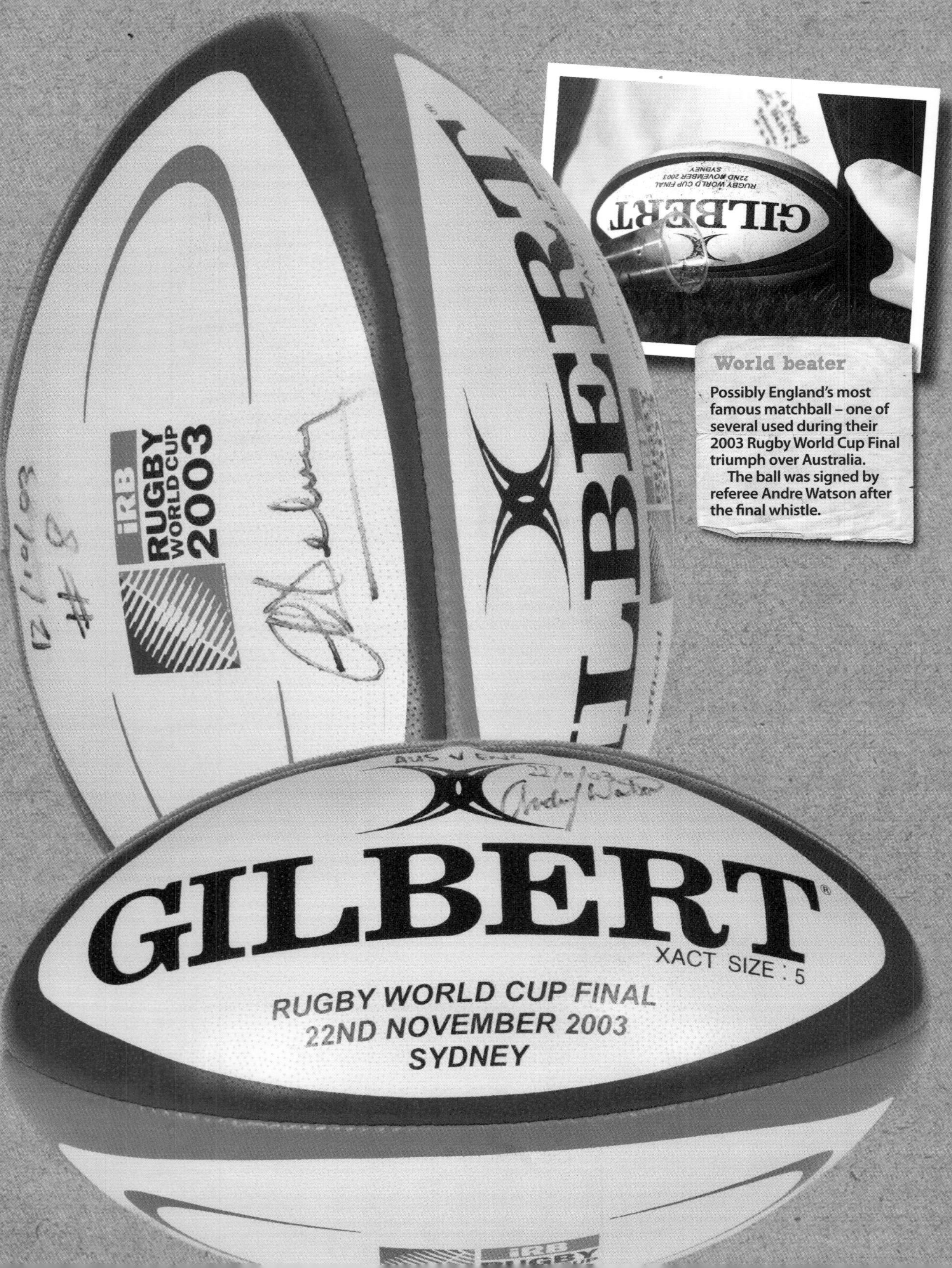

RUGBY
WORLD CUP
2003

GILBERT

GILBERT

**World beater**

Possibly England's most
famous matchball – one of
several used during their
2003 Rugby World Cup Final
triumph over Australia.
   The ball was signed by
referee Andre Watson after
the final whistle.

# GILBERT®

XACT SIZE : 5

RUGBY WORLD CUP FINAL
22ND NOVEMBER 2003
SYDNEY

# Gilbert ball facts

## The development stage

Gilbert are the official ball supplier to the Rugby World Cup 2015, and there will be a new ball developed for the tournament. There is no difference between a ball for the Rugby World Cup and a ball for the Aviva Premiership or Super Rugby competition in the southern hemisphere – Gilbert provide the same ball to each of these competitions – only the external markings are different.

## Feeling the pressure

The internal pressure of the ball is governed by the IRB. Having a consistent level of pressure inside the ball provides a more consistent product. An international standard pressure means all games start with a similar ball, which is beneficial to players.

GILBERT
SIZE : 5
MATCHBALL
VIRTUO
ENGLAND RUGBY

## Material possession

Balls are made from laminations of poly-cotton, and have a layer of rubber which creates the outer surface. The rubber is vulcanised using a mould plate, which imparts the pimples into the rubber surface – this gives the balls better grip in wet conditions.

## Rigorous testing

Balls are tested in three ways. Mechanically, using a pneumatic kicking leg; internally, using a former player – ex-England fly-half Paul Grayson; and externally, using players from around the world. Gilbert test balls to ensure that any changes to the ball provide positive results.

## Sewing things up

Gilbert rugby matchballs are hand stitched, using high quality nylon thread. Panels are stitched together using a double lock technique, to provide strong stitching, which lock together, to control the shape of the ball.

## Printing process

Logos are added onto the ball using a transfer film. The film is printed with rubber based inks, then laid onto the rubber surface. During vulcanisation, the ink cures onto the rubber, and the transfer film is then peeled off.

# OFF THE BALL

**Possession is everything in rugby, but to gain the upper hand you need strength in numbers - a philosophy which binds the successful England teams of the past and makes them masters of the scrum...**

# Forward Thinking

With 54 caps in the front row to his name, England Forwards Coach Graham Rowntree can safely claim to know something about the art of scrummaging.

It is an element of the game that continues to motivate and fascinate him, and the 2003 Grand Slam winner is in the perfect position to pass on his vast experience to England's new breed of players.

»

"I regard the English scrum as a legacy, and as a responsibility for me and the lads who play there," he said.

"It's a part of the fabric of English rugby that we have to maintain, though there are many tools available for how you play the game as a forward pack.

"What I want is an immaculate scrum, by which I mean no resets, no penalties conceded, front-foot ball for the backs and as a weapon to show our strength."

England have always looked at the scrum as an opportunity to dominate opponents and although other international sides, particularly those from the southern hemisphere, place less emphasis on its importance, Rowntree disagrees.

"It's a good tool to wear the opposition down," he added.

"But I don't want to be drawn into scrummaging the life out of people. I want guys who can do that but also play dynamically and defend smartly so that they're not a liability in defence.

"Forwards, unlike in my day, have to be good at lots of things. I was good at one thing: pushing. Hence the ears.

"These players are great specimens, and I admire the diligence they put into the game.

"I played at 16 or 16-plus stone, but we have guys now who are 19 stone and even wings pushing 16. You need some specific talent in a team but you need workers to provide the ball as well. I was one. In cycling, I'd have been a domestique.

"I'm proud of that because there's also a craft to being one of those workers. It's talent that gets you to the top, character that keeps you there, and we need a combination of both."

'I REGARD THE ENGLISH SCRUM AS A LEGACY, AND AS A RESPONSIBILITY FOR ME AND THE LADS WHO PLAY THERE. IT'S PART OF THE FABRIC OF ENGLISH RUGBY THAT WE HAVE TO MAINTAIN.'

- Graham Rowntree

THE ENGLAND SCRUM

"TOM YOUNGS AND DAN COLE ARE ALWAYS KEEN TO GET OUT THERE AND SET STANDARDS. THEY NEVER MAKE A FUSS AND THEY ALWAYS GIVE 100 PER CENT. I'D PUT MYSELF AS A PRETTY GOOD TRAINER AS WELL, THOUGH. IF YOU'RE NOT MAD FOR IT AT THIS LEVEL, YOU'RE NEVER GOING TO MAKE IT. YOU'LL GET FOUND OUT."

MY
ENGLAND
GEOFF PARLING

MY
ENGLAND
DAN COLE

"Playing in the front row is demanding but you get out of it what you put into it, so you kind of make it as hard as you want it to be.

If you want to be the best and if you want to play for England, then you have to push yourself to go further. If you have a bad day, you can either sulk and go backwards or you can get on and do what needs to be done. Plus your body adapts to the demands if you train hard and then you can push on further.

And there's also the whole teamwork thing. You're doing your best and you don't want to let your team-mates down. And you have to keep it all in perspective. I'm not going down a coal mine every day so my life really isn't all that tough, is it?"

# AWAY DAYS

**Many of England's most memorable triumphs have been on foreign soil. Whether in the northern hemisphere or southern, the Red Rose nation has long proven to be a global force...**

## FRANCE 10 ENGLAND 19

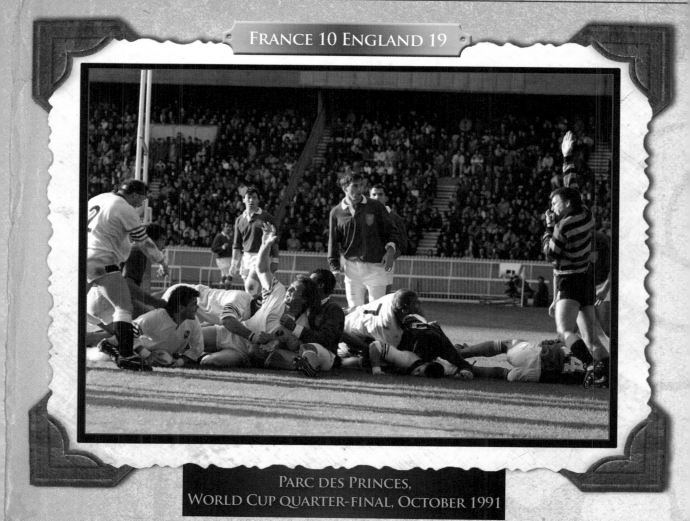

### PARC DES PRINCES,
### WORLD CUP QUARTER-FINAL, OCTOBER 1991

A truly great Anglo-French confrontation – and it certainly was a confrontation – produced one of the most famous England wins away from home.

The tone was set early when Serge Blanco lost his cool after being tackled collecting a high ball and repeatedly struck Nigel Heslop, who was left dazed on the floor.

During the early exchanges, Jeremy Guscott punched a hole in the French defence from a line-out, creating a try for Rory Underwood as England took an early lead.

It was 10-6 at the break but France came back with a try from Jean-Baptiste Lafond, which, with the conversion missed, left the scores level at 10-10.

The momentum was with the hosts until Mick Skinner's magnificent hit on Marc Cecillon at a five-metre scrum. As he dumped Cecillon on his backside, an emphatic statement had been made.

Jonathan Webb landed a penalty from distance to edge England into a 13-10 lead before, in the final minute, captain Will Carling sealed a stunning victory with an opportunist try. The win took England to the semi-final where Scotland awaited.

## AUSTRALIA 22 ENGLAND 25

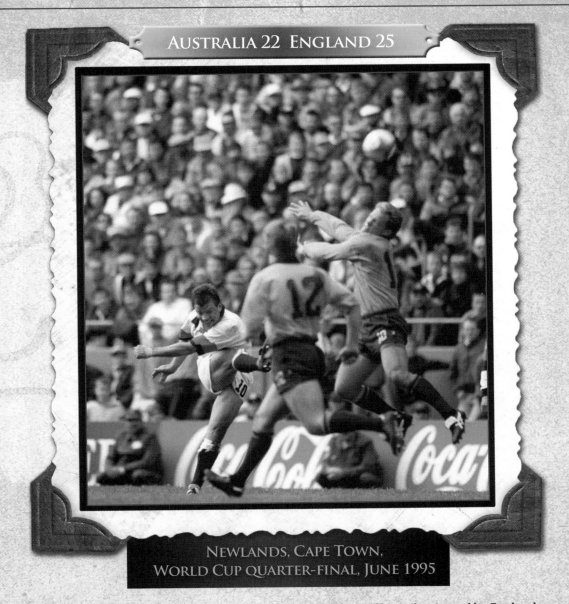

### NEWLANDS, CAPE TOWN,
### WORLD CUP QUARTER-FINAL, JUNE 1995

Jonny Wilkinson wasn't the first to land a last-minute drop-goal against the Australians in the World Cup.

The 1995 quarter-final was settled by Rob Andrew's sweetly-struck effort from over 40 metres after Martin Bayfield claimed a line-out and the pack drove forward within range.

The team, managed by Jack Rowell, had just won the Grand Slam but progress through the group stage was stuttering with unconvincing performances against Argentina, Italy and Western Samoa.

The first half was dominated by England, who scored the game's first try through Tony Underwood after breaking out from deep in their own half. With Andrew landing the conversion, the lead was 13-6.

Early in the second half the Wallabies struck back, Damian Smith touching down and Michael Lynagh's conversion levelling matters at 13-13.

Penalties were exchanged between Andrew and Lynagh until the score was 22-22, when the England fly-half struck the killer blow, taking his side through to a semi-final with New Zealand.

## IRELAND 6 ENGLAND 42

LANSDOWNE ROAD, DUBLIN,
SIX NATIONS CHAMPIONSHIP, MARCH 2003

Both teams were going for the Grand Slam but it was England who prevailed in style courtesy of a ruthlessly professional performance.

Ireland actually took an early lead thanks to a David Humphreys drop-goal but England took the lead when, after overpowering an Irish scrum, Matt Dawson ran towards the line before handing on to Lawrence Dallaglio to go under the posts.

The score was still 13-6 with almost an hour played but some daylight was established when Mike Tindall broke through the Irish defence and barged over the line.

As England now established control, Will Greenwood was driven over after his initial run was halted. The centre added another try when he intercepted a Dennis Hickie pass and sauntered over the line.

A final flourish was provided when the ball was passed through a series of hands to allow Dan Luger to score on the right wing.

## AUSTRALIA 17 ENGLAND 20

TELSTRA STADIUM, SYDNEY, AUSTRALIA
WORLD CUP FINAL, NOVEMBER 2003

The day of days for English rugby.

In the 100th minute of an exhausting, emotional evening, Jonny Wilkinson landed the drop-goal that allowed Martin Johnson to lift the William Webb Ellis trophy.

England, the pre-match favourites, certainly did it that hard way. It was Australia who struck first as Lote Tuqiri outjumped Jason Robinson after Stephen Larkham kicked a hanging high ball into the left corner. Elton Flatley's conversion attempt struck the post.

England didn't panic and gradually established control, Wilkinson kicking three penalties to take his side to a 9-5 lead.

Two minutes from half-time, Lawrence Dallaglio made a burst from midfield, passing inside to Wilkinson who in turn flung wide to Jason Robinson; the wing put his head down and sped over in the left-hand corner, joyously punching the ball in celebration.

A 14-5 half-time lead and England seemed well set but, as basic errors crept in, Australia gradually chipped away and a last-minute Flatley penalty brought the scores level at 14-14.

Early in extra-time, Wilkinson landed a long-distance penalty but, once again with time running out, Flatley kicked a penalty of his own to make it 17-17.

With sudden death looming, England kept their composure and executed a move that is now imprinted in our minds: Lewis Moody won a line-out, Mike Catt, Matt Dawson and Martin Johnson drove forward and it was set up for Wilkinson to send a right-footed drop-goal between the posts to win the World Cup with less than 30 seconds remaining.

# The GROWING Game

From grassroots to the international stage, the Varsity Match to rugby sevens, the oval game has developed considerably over the years. The high profile of the women's game, together with increased youth development, is helping shape an even brighter future, one which continues to regale fans and royalty alike

# MY ENGLAND
## LAWRENCE DALLAGLIO

"The RFU are the gatekeepers of rugby in this country. They run the game in England, and when we talk about the game, we don't just mean the elite professional game, but everything. The professional game is really quite small and we only have two fully professional leagues in this country, but they are responsible for women's rugby, grassroots rugby, junior level etc and they have a huge mandate.

They clearly want to see more people coming through and playing and watching rugby and making more players eligible to play for England. Ultimately, the 82,000 who come and watch England on a regular basis come from the grassroots of the game and the RFU continue to work with young, disadvantaged kids and people from lots and lots of different areas.

My charity, The Dallaglio Foundation, have just partnered with the RFU to work with disadvantaged young children in areas all over the country, and with the World Cup taking place here in 2015, that gives us a chance to grow the game further and I think that will change the landscape of rugby in this country.

It is our responsibility to make sure that doesn't just happen in 2015, but that it starts now and its important that the values of rugby that so encapsulate the game are shown not only in the national side, but throughout the whole sport."

# The Varsity Match

The Varsity Match is one of rugby union's most historic fixtures, having first been played in 1872, just a year after the first international, between England and Scotland, was held.

Cambridge and Oxford universities have played each other annually ever since, save for interruptions caused by the two world wars.

The inaugural match was played at The Parks, Oxford, a 20-a-side encounter won by Oxford, before the second fixture took place at Parker's Piece in Cambridge.

Since then, London has always been the venue. The Oval in Kennington staged seven fixtures; it moved to two venues in Blackheath before finding a regular home between 1887 and 1920 at the Queen's Club, Kensington, which is now more associated with tennis.

From 1921, Twickenham has staged every Varsity Match, which is traditionally played in December and remains a major social and sporting occasion.

Over 600 players to have featured over the years have won international honours, including New Zealand's World Cup-winning captain in 1987, David Kirk, plus Rob Andrew, Stuart Barnes, Gavin Hastings, Joe Roff, Tony Underwood and Paul Ackford.

Following the 131st fixture in 2012, Cambridge had claimed 61 victories, Oxford 56 and there have been 14 draws.

CAMBRIDGE PROP

D. BRETT

CAMBRIDGE UNIVERSITY R.U.F.C.

FOUNDED 1872

BLOCK V EAST STAND

Entrance to Block at back of Stand Entrance to Ground, Rugby Road

Row 17 Seat 348

Oxford v. Cambridge

AT TWICKENHAM

TUESDAY, DEC. 9th, 1924. Kick-off 2.30 p.m.

Price - 7/6

S. F. COOPPER.

OXFORD FLANKER

L. SHERR

OXFORD UNIVERSITY R.F.C.

FOUNDED 1869

GILBERT

LEHMAN BROTHER

WINNERS

## All-round Success

Twickenham may be at its loudest during an England international, but the venue is also used by various other teams and organisations throughout the year.

Women's rugby continues to go from strength to strength, at both grassroots and international level, with 14,000 women registered by the RFU and the England side among the strongest in the world.

The RFU's Women's and Girls' Player Pathway is determined to see women's rugby thrive in England and offers women the opportunity to progress from club rugby all the way through to the national side.

On certain occasions, England Women's games take place immediately after their male counterparts have played and that gives the sport a great opportunity to showcase the incredible skills and athleticism in the female game.

It helps when you are a successful

side as well, and continued Six Nations success – plus recent dominance over New Zealand – means the women's game continues to grow apace.

Twickenham also gets used extensively by domestic and amateur sides.

At the top of the professional game, the Premiership final is contested at Twickenham while Heineken Cup games have also been frequently played at the ground.

Part-time players get the chance to show off their skills at Twickenham as the County Championship holds its showcase final at the ground.

First played in 1889, the tournament splits counties into north and south and the winner of each respective section then compete for the Bill Beaumont Cup.

Lancashire have won the competition 21 times with Gloucestershire (17) and Yorkshire (15) in hot pursuit.

A host of sevens tournaments have also called Twickenham home with the Marriott London Sevens attracting crowds off 100,000 over the weekend while the Daily Mail RBS Cup, now the Natwest Schools Cup, gives school pupils a once-in-a-lifetime opportunity to play at the home of rugby.

RFU President, Paul Murphy, said: "Twickenham Stadium hosts a variety of matches from the England Tests to the Army v Navy match for the Babcock Trophy; Schools Day; the British Universities and Colleges Finals; the Bill Beaumont Cup Final and County Championship Shield Final.

"Each has its particular atmosphere but for a player running out for their club on RFU Cup Finals day in May, the occasion is a special as for an England international taking on another nation."

# Fan Power

England fans flock to Twickenham, and every other corner of the globe, whenever the national side play

West London gets turned into a red and white calvacade as the home of rugby fills up with supporters from all over the country, desperate to see England prosper.

Each St George's flag and every chorus of 'Swing Low Sweet Chariot' undoubtedly helps push England's players harder, faster and further.

Stuart Lancaster said: "English rugby fans are hugely passionate. They care about the team and they want to get behind the team. The players respect that and they really want to give the supporters something to shout about.

"It's important to make supporters feel proud of the England team and for them to see that we appreciate them."

The England rugby team have been world champions on just one occasion; but their supporters are world champions every single time England run out onto the field.

## THE ENGLAND FANS

## MY ENGLAND
### LAWRENCE DALLAGLIO

"The crowd are your extra man. The roar is amazing and it's an amazing feeling. England fans are deeply passionate. I come from an Italian background with a little bit of Irish and I always say that makes me a dangerous Englishman and I've always felt that connection with the supporters.

I remember coming through the West Car Park which was the traditional entrance for the team and you get hit with a wall of noise. Fans line the streets from Whitton all the way through to Twickenham and that used to make the hairs on your neck stand up because you got a real connection with the fans."

# Royal rapport

From King George V's attendance at England's first game at Twickenham in 1910 to Prince Harry's current interest in developing youth rugby, the RFU has always attracted Royal interest.

Harry, who is the RFU's Vice-Patron, takes a huge interest in the sport and was famously invited into the dressing room in Sydney following England's 2003 World Cup victory.

He is also currently a patron of the RFU's All Schools programme which is aiming to get rugby union played in more secondary schools up and down the country.

And plenty of other Royals have also been spotted at Twickenham on matchday.

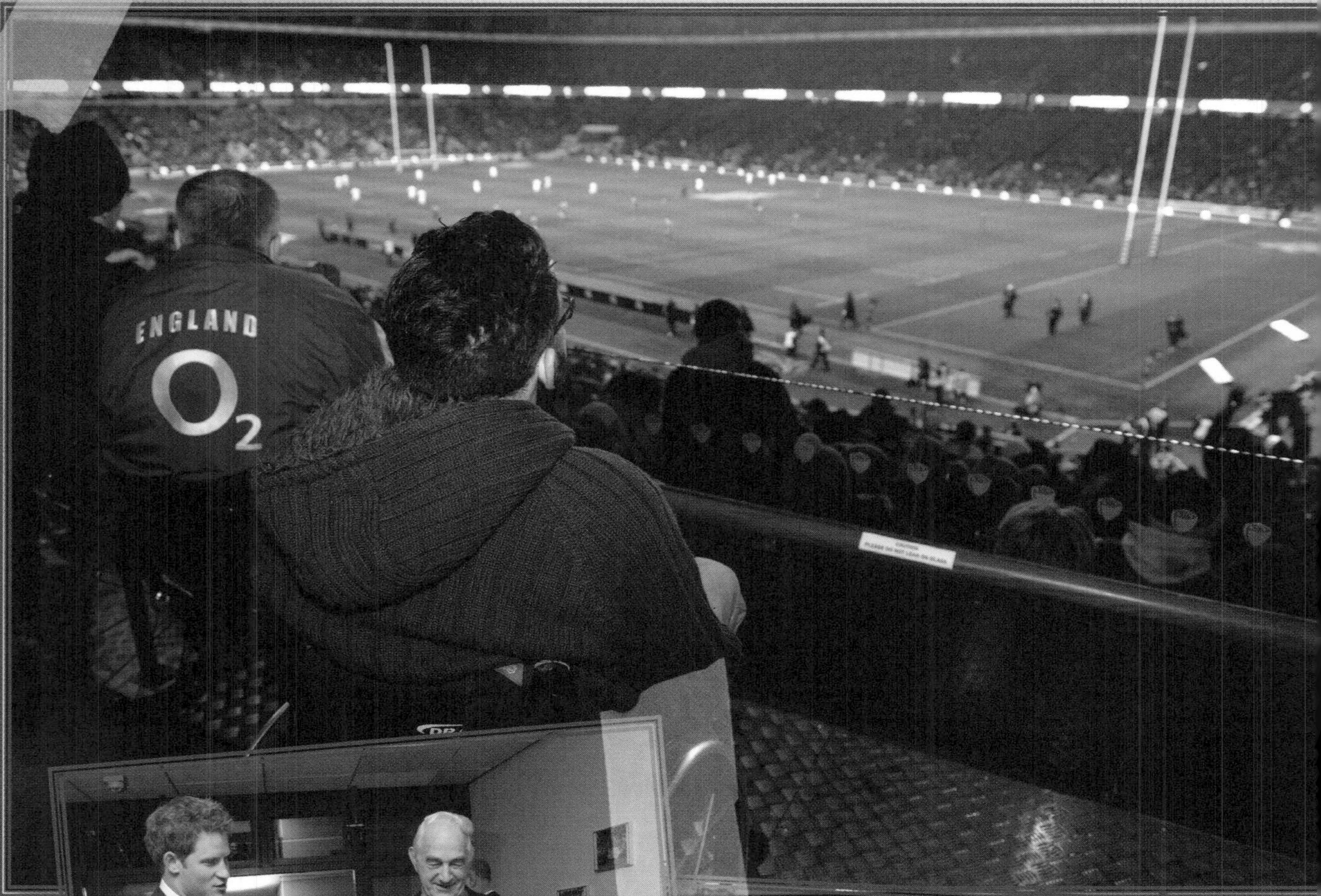
ENGLAND
O2

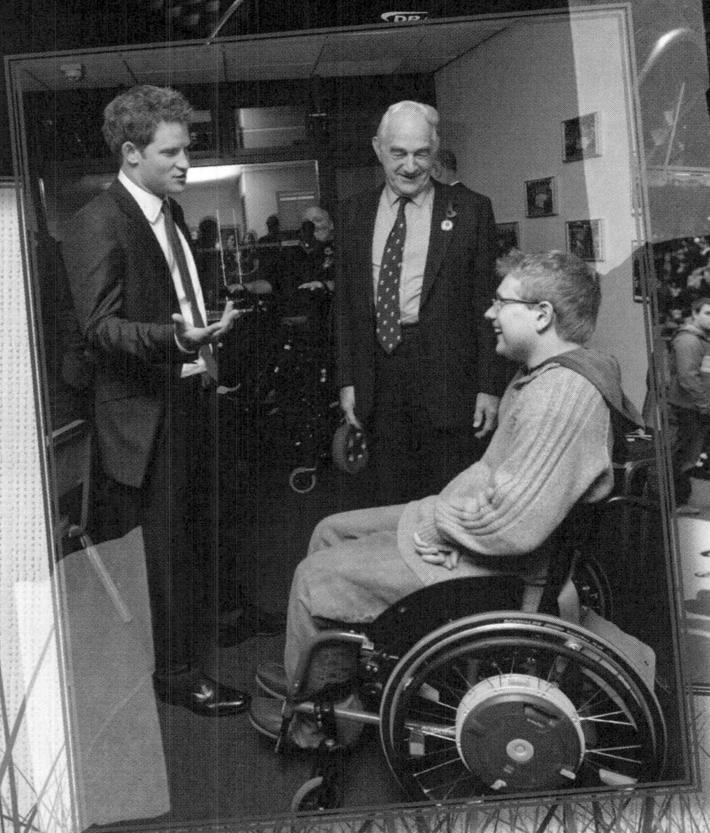

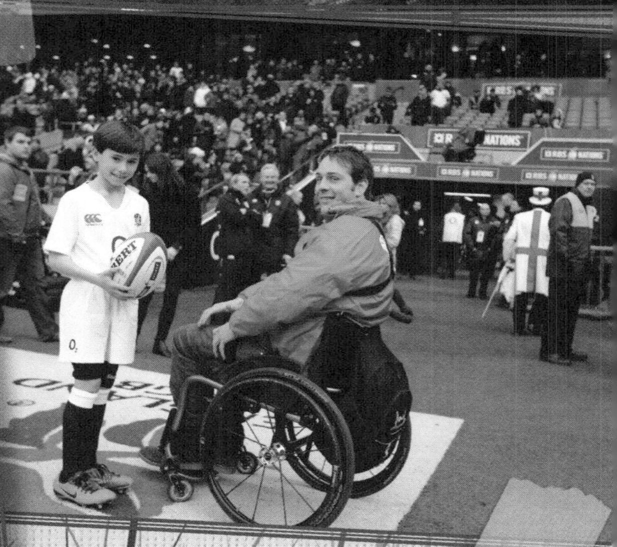

# Injured Players Foundation

Twickenham has witnessed many incredible sights and seen many heroic deeds.

And the work of the Injured Players Foundation (IPF) deserves its place alongside – and perhaps above – all of them.

Occasionally a rugby player, either amateur or professional, will receive a serious and life changing injury, and when that happens, the IPF is there to help.

The IPF provides emotional, financial and practical support to any player seriously injured.

The organisation gives fresh hope, arranges vital medical help and raises spirits.

Every injured player receives as much help as is required in order to give them as many chances as possible to return to a full and fulfilling life.

Every injured player knows that there is someone there for them – in person, on the end of a phone and everywhere in between.

They are also offered an exclusive opportunity every two years to visit Twickenham for an international occasion and a specially designed box gives any members of the IPF an unrivalled view of the pitch.

Those injured playing rugby continue to love the game and the state-of-the-art IPF box allows all its members the chance to cheer on their heroes like everybody else.

Karen Hood, IPF Medical Manager, said: "The IPF covers everything from going to the hospital as soon as the injury has taken place, to carrying out educational projects to try and lessen the chances of a traumatic injury taking place.

"We try and do everything we can to help people and it is nice to see and hear the positive impact that our work can have.

"The RFU steps in and helps in whatever way is needed, whether that be financially, practically, emotionally or all three of them.

"We try to lift the burden, organise any physio and do everything we can to alleviate the effects of what are truly life-changing injuries."

ENGLAND

*Photographs*

Legendary England captain Wavell Wakefield and France
counterpart Aime Cassayet-Armagnac reflect on their Five
Nations encounter at Twickenham, which England won 19-7.
The Red Rose side followed this up with a 19-0 victory over
Scotland to seal the Grand Slam, their second in succession

England and Harlequins centre William Davies touches down for the British and Irish Lions during their tour of South Africa in 1955

Fran Cotton, England's new captain, helps team-mate Keith Fairbrother at his Coventry fruit and veg stall in 1975

Rory Underwood takes a breather as England beat Wales 21-18 at Twickenham in 1986

Bill Beaumont leads an England charge against France at Twickenham in 1977

England prepare for the 1975 tour of Australia with some training drills at Lensbury Club, Teddington

Time for some scrum practice as England train at Roehampton in 1978

Andrew Sheridan and Matt Dunning square up during the 2007 Rugby World Cup quarter-final encounter at the Stade Velodrome, France

Matt Dawson goes over the line against Wales in 2001

Brian Moore gets ready for battle in 1991

England do some fine tuning ahead of their Twickenham meeting with Australia in January 1976

Lawrence Dallaglio shows immense strength to power through the Wales defence for a try as England win 46–12 at Twickenham during the 2000 Six Nations campaign

The England squad put in a few laps of their Coventry training ground in February 1979

England winger David Duckham suits up for his office job in 1974

199

The 1924
England team

Former England coach and RFU president John Burgess gives some orders in November 1972

Newly-appointed England captain Steve Smith gets to grips with Bill Beaumont in February 1982

The famous 'Ghost in the Painting' portrait which hangs on the wall of the President's Suite at Twickenham. It shows a late 19th century Roses battle between Lancashire and Yorkshire. A ghostly figure is visible in the centre, although this phantom effect stems from an apparent attempt to remove a player who had turned professional

Steve Smith training between lessons at Carlett Park
College, Eastham, in January 1973

England pose for a team photograph during the 1955 Five Nations Championship

Dean Richards and Gareth Chilcott show some alternative fancy footwork with the English National Ballet in 2000

Chris Ashton's famous flying finish as he goes over for a try during England's 2011 World Cup victory over Georgia

Man mountain Fran Cotton during a training session in 1974

FOOTBALL RULES.

# RFU Timeline

**All the key dates and events surrounding the creation of the game and the establishment of its home at Twickenham...**

## 1820-1829

## 1830-1839

### 1823
Rugby School pupil William Webb Ellis supposedly picks up a football and runs, thus creating the game of rugby. However, the story is widely believed to be apocryphal.

### 1839
Students at Cambridge University argue over different sets of rules for playing football.

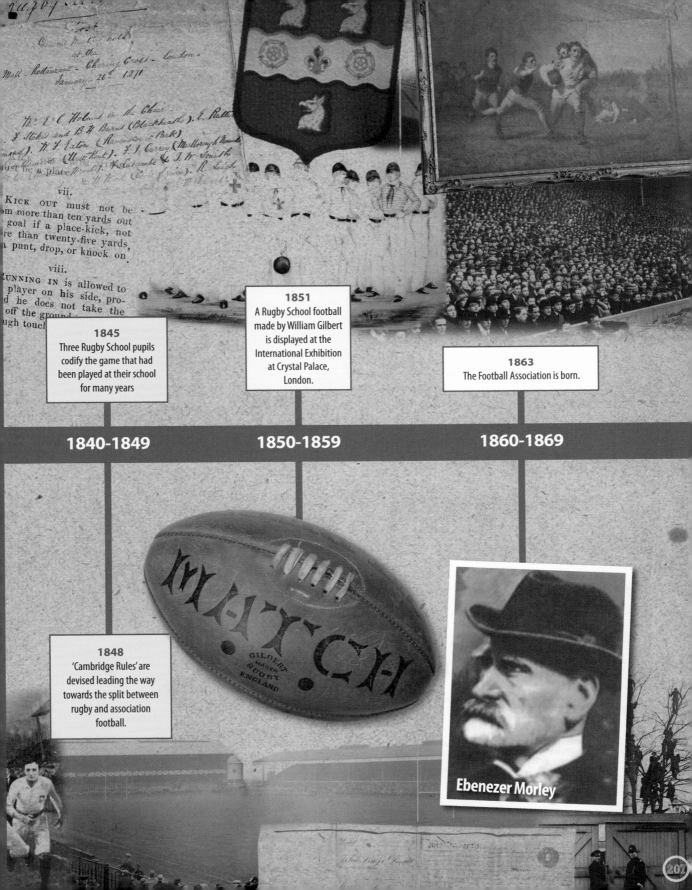

**1845**
Three Rugby School pupils codify the game that had been played at their school for many years

**1851**
A Rugby School football made by William Gilbert is displayed at the International Exhibition at Crystal Palace, London.

**1863**
The Football Association is born.

**1840-1849**

**1850-1859**

**1860-1869**

**1848**
'Cambridge Rules' are devised leading the way towards the split between rugby and association football.

**Ebenezer Morley**

# RFU Timeline

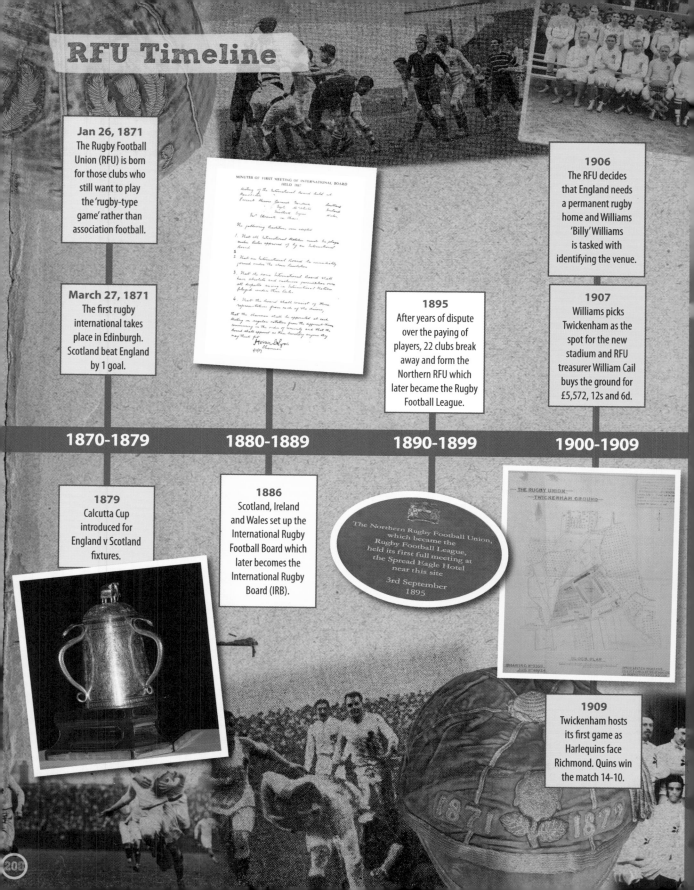

**Jan 26, 1871**
The Rugby Football Union (RFU) is born for those clubs who still want to play the 'rugby-type game' rather than association football.

**March 27, 1871**
The first rugby international takes place in Edinburgh. Scotland beat England by 1 goal.

**1895**
After years of dispute over the paying of players, 22 clubs break away and form the Northern RFU which later became the Rugby Football League.

**1906**
The RFU decides that England needs a permanent rugby home and Williams 'Billy' Williams is tasked with identifying the venue.

**1907**
Williams picks Twickenham as the spot for the new stadium and RFU treasurer William Cail buys the ground for £5,572, 12s and 6d.

**1870-1879**   **1880-1889**   **1890-1899**   **1900-1909**

**1879**
Calcutta Cup introduced for England v Scotland fixtures.

**1886**
Scotland, Ireland and Wales set up the International Rugby Football Board which later becomes the International Rugby Board (IRB).

The Northern Rugby Football Union, which became the Rugby Football League, held its first full meeting at the Spread Eagle Hotel near this site

3rd September 1895

**1909**
Twickenham hosts its first game as Harlequins face Richmond. Quins win the match 14-10.

**1920**
England beat France 8-3 in the first match at Twickenham in six years following the outbreak of World War I.

**1921**
The Varsity Match takes place at Twickenham for the first time as Oxford beat Cambridge 11-5.

**1924**
England earn a fifth clean sweep after a 19-0 victory against Scotland.

**1932**
The new West Stand is completed and the South Terrace is also extended.

**1936**
Prince Alexander Obolensky scores two brilliant tries as England record their first victory over the All Blacks at Twickenham.

**1913**

**1910**
England play their first international at Twickenham, winning 11-6 against Wales with King George V in attendance.

## 1910-1919

## 1920-1929

## 1930-1939

## 1940-1949

**1913**
England win their first Grand Slam as they beat Scotland 3-0.

**1914**
Further Grand Slam glory is achieved as England underline their pre-war strength.

**1925**
The new North Stand is opened – taking Twickenham's capacity to over 60,000.

**1926**
England suffer their first Five Nations home defeat, losing to Scotland 17-9.

**1927**
The BBC's first ever live sporting broadcast takes place at Twickenham as England take on Wales.

**1928**
Australia play their first game at Twickenham but lose 18-11.

**1938**
The BBC show live coverage of a Twickenham match for the first time as Scotland beat England 21-16.

**1939**
World War II puts Twickenham on hold for five years as the ground is used as a coal dump and also dug up for allotments to aid the war effort.

**1945**
Rugby restarts as an England XV are beaten 18-3 by a New Zealand Army Touring XV.

# RFU Timeline

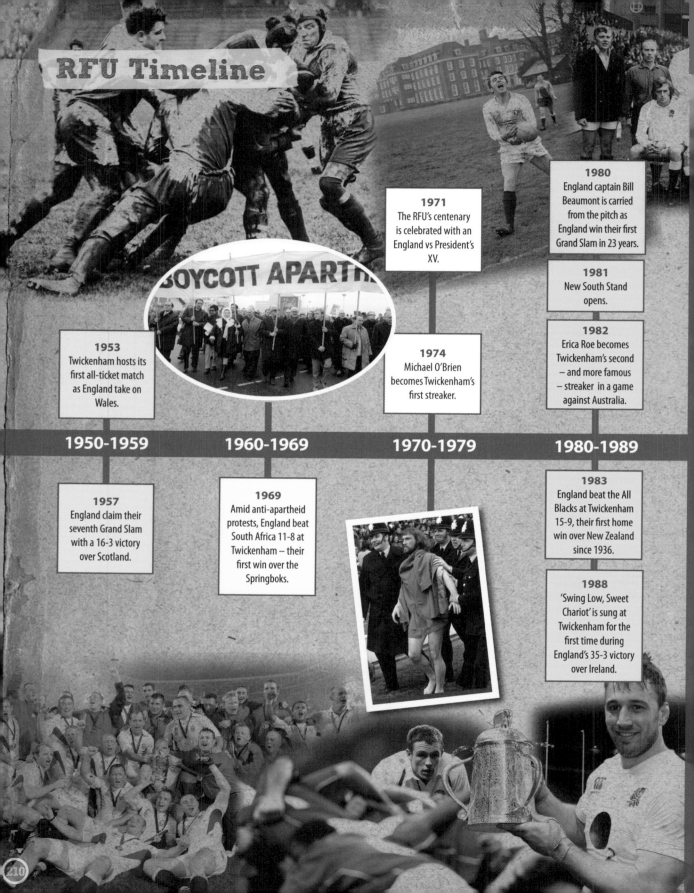

**1971**
The RFU's centenary is celebrated with an England vs President's XV.

**1980**
England captain Bill Beaumont is carried from the pitch as England win their first Grand Slam in 23 years.

**1981**
New South Stand opens.

**1953**
Twickenham hosts its first all-ticket match as England take on Wales.

**1974**
Michael O'Brien becomes Twickenham's first streaker.

**1982**
Erica Roe becomes Twickenham's second – and more famous – streaker in a game against Australia.

**1950-1959**     **1960-1969**     **1970-1979**     **1980-1989**

**1957**
England claim their seventh Grand Slam with a 16-3 victory over Scotland.

**1969**
Amid anti-apartheid protests, England beat South Africa 11-8 at Twickenham – their first win over the Springboks.

**1983**
England beat the All Blacks at Twickenham 15-9, their first home win over New Zealand since 1936.

**1988**
'Swing Low, Sweet Chariot' is sung at Twickenham for the first time during England's 35-3 victory over Ireland.

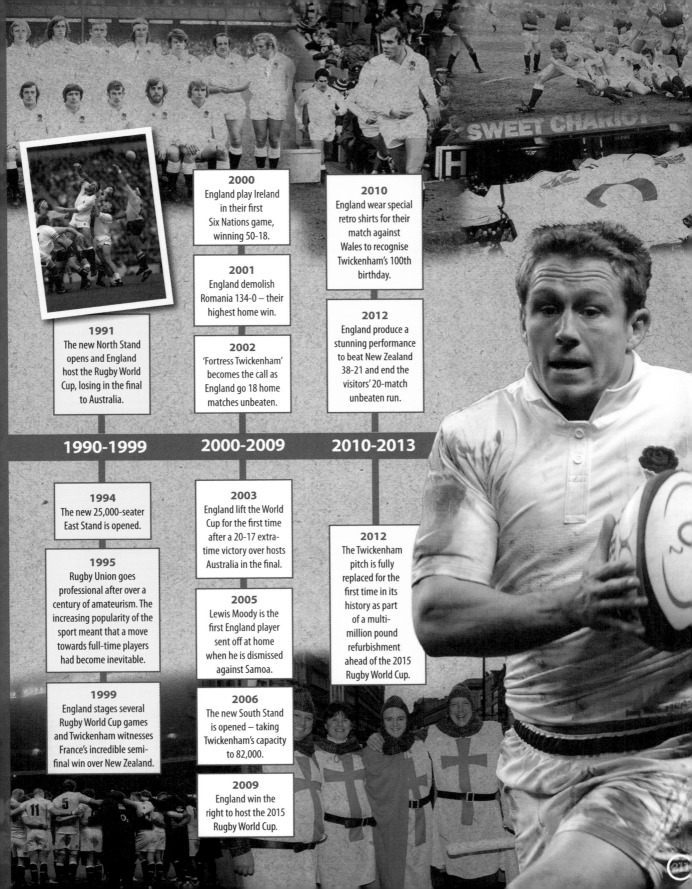

**2000**
England play Ireland in their first Six Nations game, winning 50-18.

**2001**
England demolish Romania 134-0 – their highest home win.

**2002**
'Fortress Twickenham' becomes the call as England go 18 home matches unbeaten.

**2010**
England wear special retro shirts for their match against Wales to recognise Twickenham's 100th birthday.

**2012**
England produce a stunning performance to beat New Zealand 38-21 and end the visitors' 20-match unbeaten run.

**1991**
The new North Stand opens and England host the Rugby World Cup, losing in the final to Australia.

## 1990-1999

## 2000-2009

## 2010-2013

**1994**
The new 25,000-seater East Stand is opened.

**1995**
Rugby Union goes professional after over a century of amateurism. The increasing popularity of the sport meant that a move towards full-time players had become inevitable.

**1999**
England stages several Rugby World Cup games and Twickenham witnesses France's incredible semi-final win over New Zealand.

**2003**
England lift the World Cup for the first time after a 20-17 extra-time victory over hosts Australia in the final.

**2005**
Lewis Moody is the first England player sent off at home when he is dismissed against Samoa.

**2006**
The new South Stand is opened – taking Twickenham's capacity to 82,000.

**2009**
England win the right to host the 2015 Rugby World Cup.

**2012**
The Twickenham pitch is fully replaced for the first time in its history as part of a multi-million pound refurbishment ahead of the 2015 Rugby World Cup.

**12 GRAND SLAMS**

**2003 WORLD CUP WINNERS**

**TOP POINTS SCORER**

**TOP TRY SCORER**

**MOST POINTS IN A MATCH**

**MOST CAPS**

**BIGGEST VICTORY**

**MOST MATCHES AS CAPTAIN**

**EXTRA TIME**
10 Minutes each way
(time out for injury)
Will commence in 5 minutes

**HIGHEST ATTENDANCE**

**MOST CONSECUTIVE HOME WINS**

**FASTEST TRY BY DEBUTANT**

**MOST CONSECUTIVE AWAY WIN**

# ENGLAND RUGBY

## HONOURS BOARD

| | |
|---|---|
| **GRAND SLAMS:** | 1913, 1914, 1921, 1923, 1924, 1928, 1957, 1980, 1991, 1992, 1995, 2003 |
| **WORLD CUP WINNERS:** | 2003 |
| **MOST POINTS:** | Jonny Wilkinson – 1179 |
| **MOST TRIES:** | Rory Underwood – 49 |
| **MOST CONVERSIONS:** | Jonny Wilkinson – 162 |
| **MOST PENALTIES:** | Jonny Wilkinson – 239 |
| **MOST DROP-GOALS:** | Jonny Wilkinson – 36 |
| **MOST TRIES IN A MATCH:** | 20 – England 134 Romania 0, Twickenham, November 2001 |
| **MOST POINTS SCORED IN A MATCH BY AN INDIVIDUAL:** | 44 – Charlie Hodgson, England 134 Romania 0, Twickenham, November 2001 |
| **MOST CAPS:** | Jason Leonard – 114 |
| **BIGGEST VICTORY:** | England 134 Romania 0, Twickenham, November 2001 |
| **MOST MATCHES AS CAPTAIN:** | Will Carling – 59 |
| **FASTEST TRY:** | Leo Price – 10 seconds v Wales, Twickenham, January 1923 |
| **FASTEST TRY BY DEBUTANT:** | Fred Chapman – 75 seconds – v Wales, January 1910 |
| **HIGHEST ATTENDANCE:** | 82,957 – Australia 17 England 20 2003 Rugby World Cup Final, Telstra Stadium, Sydney |
| **MOST CONSECUTIVE WINS:** | 14 – March 23, 2002 v Wales – Aug 23, 2003 v Wales. |
| **MOST CONSECUTIVE HOME WINS:** | 22 – Oct 15, 1999 v Tonga – Sep 6, 2003 v France |
| **MOST CONSECUTIVE AWAY WINS:** | 9 – Oct 12, 2003 v Georgia – Feb 21, 2004 v Scotland |
| **OLDEST APPEARANCE:** | 39 years – Frederick Gilbert, v Ireland, Feb 10, 1923 |
| **YOUNGEST APPEARANCE:** | 18 years 124 days – Colin Laird, v Wales, Jan 15, 1927 |

TWICKENHAM
WALL OF FAME

ALEXANDER OBOLENSKY
ENGLAND

FRANCOIS PIENAAR
SOUTH AFRICA

MASSIMO GIOVANELLI
ITALY

NORMAN WODEHOUSE
ENGLAND

COLIN MEADS
NEW ZEALAND

IN HASTINGS
SCOTLAND

DEAN RICHARDS
ENGLAND

JK JOHN MCBRIDE
IRELAND

PETER WINTERBOTTOM
ENGLAND

KEN CATCHPOLE
AUSTRALIA

WILLIE CROIGHDEAN
IRELAND

LEWIS JONES
WALES

# Wall Of Fame

**ROB ANDREW • NEIL BACK • BILL BEAUMONT • JOHN BIRKETT • JEFF BUTTERFIELD • WILL CARLING • FE CHAPMAN • FRAN COTTON • DR COVE-SMITH • LAWRENCE DALLAGLIO • WJA DAVIES • WADE DOOLEY • DAVID DUCKHAM • ERIC EVANS • BERNARD GADNEY • JEREMY GUSCOTT • RICHARDHILL • BOB HILLER • PETER JACKSON • RON JACOBS • DICKIE JEEPS • MARTIN JOHNSON • JASON LEONARD • CYRIL LOWE • BRIAN MOORE • ALEXANDER OBOLENSKY • CHRIS OTI • RONALD POULTON-PALMER • DEAN RICHARDS • JASONROBINSON • BUDGE ROGERS • HAL SEVER • RICHARD SHARP • ADRIAN STOOP • RORY UNDERWOOD • ROGER UTTLEY • W W WAKEFIELD • PETER WHEELER • PETER WINTERBOTTOM • NORMAN WODEHOUSE • CLIVE WOODWARD**

*The England players all feature as part of 'The Wall of Fame', opened at the World Rugby Museum (formally Museum of Rugby) by Martin Johnson on 3rd June, 2005, with the final players being inducted in 2010 at the stadium's centenary. For further information visit* **rfu.com/museum**

# The Scroll Of Honour

*Compiled from loyal fans who subscribed to*
*The Official England Rugby Scrapbook*

# OUR FANS A-E

DANIEL ALLAWAY • JUDITH ALLAWAY • TERESA ALLAWAY • THOMAS ALLAWAY • JAQUELINE ARMITAGE • NATALIE ARMITAGE • NICHOLAS ARMITAGE • PHILIP ARMITAGE • CURTLEY BALE • EMILY JOANNA BAMBRIDGE • AARON BARKER • LUKE BARLOW • LUKE BARLOW • NATHAN BARLOW • RAY BARLOW • EILEEN BARR • KYLE BARR • YZELLA BARR • LIAM BARRON • FREDERIC BARRY • LAURENCE BARRY • OLIVER BARRY • ARWEN BARTLETT • ISABELLE BARTLETT • LANA BARTLETT • PAIGE BARTLETT • BERTY BEAR • CLARE BERRY • DAWN BEZUS • JOEL BEZUS • MICHAEL BEZUS • DEAN BIBBY • JANE BIBBY • JOE BIBBY • CHRISTINA BIGGS • PATRICIA BIGGS • STEVEN BIGGS • RON BIGGS (IN MEMORY) • ALEX BILLMAN • BILLY BILLMAN • MICK BILLMAN • JACK BINCER • ALAN BLACKFORD • ANN BLUNDELL • PAULINE BOLAM • ADRIAN BOLD • KIM BOLD • NICK BOLD • SAM BOLD • JO BOOTH • EMMA BRADLEY • ERIC BRADLEY • GARY BRAME • IAN BROOKER • THE BROOKER FAMILY • ELLIE BROWN • VRENY BROWN • ALAN BROWNING • ANTHONY BROWNING • ELLIS BULLARD • HARRY BULLARD • VINCE BURFORD • KATHERINE CARROLL • NIAMH CARROLL • COZY CAT • DOREEN CHALMERS • RUTH CHAMBERS • ANDREW CHEESEMAN • DAVID PETER CHEESEMAN • EMMA NONDE CHEESEMAN • JANET CHEESEMAN • JONATHAN MILES CHEESEMAN • NICHOLAS GUY CHEESEMAN • SUSAN ELISABETH CHEESEMAN • CHLOE CHING • JULIAN CHING • MICHAEL CHING • SARAH CHING • DAVID COCKERILL • PAUL COCKERILL • TIM COLES • DAVID COLLINS • KIM CONSTANTINE • PETER CONSTANTINE • FIONA COPE • JAMES COPLAND • JESSICA COPLAND • MARIE COPLAND • PETER COPLAND • MIKE COSTERTON • FRANCESCA COXON • FRANCES CROUCH • JOHN CROUCH • JOHN CRUDDAS • LYNN CRUDDAS • TONY CRUDDAS • ZOE DAGLISH • MICHAEL DALY • JAMES JM DARGAN • RICHARD DAVIES • TONY DICKENSON • ELVIN DOYLE • PATRICK FORBES DOYLE • BENJAMIN DREW • DAVID DREW • GREGORY DREW • JIM DUBERRY • JO DUNGEY • RICHARD W EARLE • PETE EATON • BENJAMIN A EDWARDS • DYLAN EDWARDS • NICKI EDWARDS • OWEN J EDWARDS •

# OUR FANS E-L

STEVE EMBERTON • FIONA EVERARD • LYNDEN FATHERS • SIMON FATHERS • TONY FATHERS • AMANDA FENNER • DARREN FENTON • JACOB FENTON • NICOLA FENTON • SAMUEL FENTON • MICHAEL FISHER • DEREK FOLEY • VINCENT FORBES • GRAHAM FORRESTER • TRACEY FORRESTER • JAMES FOSTER • JOSETTE FOSTER • DAVID FOULDS • ISLA FOULDS • LOU FOULDS • ROSS FOULDS • ADAM FRANCIS • DAVID FREEMAN • DAWN PAMELA GALLAGHER • JASON GARDNER • SUE GARDNER • AMY GARNER • JOHN GARNER • PHILIP GARNER • SHARON GARNER • ANDY GIBSON • RICHARD GILBERT • TINA GILBERT • ANN GISBORNE • DANIEL GISBORNE • JAMES GISBORNE • NEAL GISBORNE • LEO GOMES • EDDIE GOODALL • MATTHEW GREENSLADE • 3D GRIL • KAREN HALL • RICHARD HALL • CHARLOTTE HAMBLIN • PAUL HAMBLIN • ROGER HAMBLIN • SOPHIA HAMBLIN • GABRIEL HAMMOND • NATHALIE HAMMOND • NICK HAMMOND • NOAH HAMMOND • BEATRICE HAMPSHIRE • NEIL HAMPSHIRE • TABITHA HAMPSHIRE • VICKIE HAMPSHIRE • JACOB HAMSHERE • JOE HAMSHERE • JOHN HAMSHERE • JOHN HAMSHERE • NIGEL HAMSHERE • PAMELA HAMSHERE • PETER HAMSHERE • MARIAN HANKS • TERRY HANKS SNR • KWANLA HANNIS • MARTIN HANNIS • ANDREW J HARDING • WILLIAM J HARDING • RAY HARRIS • CHARLIE HODGSON • PETER WILLIAM HOLLAND • SANDRA AGNES HOLLAND • ADAM HOPKINS • DANIEL HOPKINS • LOTTIE HOPKINS • SUSAN HOPKINS • ROBERT JAMES HORE • ROGER HORE • TAYLOR JAMES HORE • DAVID HOWELL • DAVID HUNT • EDWARD HUNT • WILLIAM HUNT • SIMON HUTTON • MARC IDE • JOHN IRVING • MARK JENKINS • MATT JENKINS • BARRY JOHNSON • BECKY JOHNSON • BRIAN JOHNSON • LORRAINE JOHNSON • RICHARD JOHNSON • BRIAN JOHNSON SNR • JOHN ROBERT JONES • KATHLEEN JONES • LAURA JONES • NATHAN DANIEL JONES • REBECCA JONES • JOHN JONES • CAMERON KENDALL • HEATHER KENDALL • STEVE KENDALL • GRACE KEYES • JACK KEYES • MICHELLE KEYES • ROGER KEYES • PETER KIMBLE • STEPHEN KIMBLE • JAMES KLINSKI • COURTNEY LAWRENCE • GEORGE LAWRENCE • LYNN LAWRENCE • PAIGE LAWRENCE • STEPHEN LEADER • JERRAD LEWIS • NIGEL LOCKYER •

# OUR FANS L-S

BETTY LOVELL • ERIC LOVELL • ISOBEL LOVELL • KARL LOVELL • ROBIN LOVELL • SALLY LOVELL • SUSAN LOVELL • GEOFFREY LUKER • MARIE LUKER • GRAHAM MACCALLUM • JACOB DAVID MARRIOTT • KERRY MARRIOTT • NAOMI DAWN MARRIOTT • REBECCA SARAH MARRIOTT • ANDREW MASI • CHRIS MASI • ETHAN MASI • LENNIE MASI • DAVE MASSEY • TINA MASSEY • MALCOLM MCCARTHY • MATT MCCARTHY • THOM EM MCCARTHY • DENNIS MCDINE • ALISTAIR IAIN MCLEAN • CELIA MEILTON • ROBIN MEILTON • SANDY MENZIES • JUDE MITCHELL • ROSIE MKRTCHYAN • CHRIS MORGAN-SMITH • HELEN MORGAN-SMITH • KERI MORGAN-SMITH • ROB MORGAN-SMITH • EVA MORLEY • JOSHUA MORLEY • KYLA MORLEY • NICHOLAS MORLEY • ISABEL MORRIS • JOHN MOYNIHAN • MARY-ANNE MOYNIHAN • JAMIE MULLENDER • JEFF MULLENDER • STEVEN MULLENDER • JANE NEAT • WILLIAM NEAT • TONY NOBILE • HEYMO NYONI • MATT OAKLEY • MARTIN OLAM • JAMES PAGE • OLIVE PAINTIN • SOPHIA PANG • JAMES PARKER • OLIVER PARKER • STEVE PARKER • TOM PARKER • CHRIS PARKER-OWLE • BRETT PEAKE • CALLUM PEAKE • MARK PEARCE • RICHARD PIGOTT • TRUDY PIGOTT • JACK POPE • JONATHAN POPE • ROY POPE • RUTH POPE • COLIN F POTT • STEVEN M POTT • DANIEL POWELL • NICHOLAS ANDREW POWELL • ROBERT EDWARD POWELL • WILLIAM BENJAMIN POWELL • EMMA VICTORIA PULLAN • DAVID LESLIE QUINN • KATIE LOUISE QUINN • LEE RAIKES • WILLIAM RAIKES • ROSEMARY REDWOOD • CAROLINE RHODES • PETE RIDLEY • TOM RIPPON • PETE ROBBINS • ANDREW ROBERTS • ANNETTE ROBERTS • BEN ROBERTS • BRONWYN ROBERTS • DAVID ROBERTS • LUCY ROBERTS • SHERIDAN ROBERTS • HARRY ELLIOT ROBINSON • PAUL JOHN ROBINSON • ROBERT JOHN ROBINSON • JOHN RUDD • ALISTAIR RUSSELL • DAISY RYDER • JOSEPH RYDER • MADELINE RYDER • MURFEY RYDER • MAGGY SADLER • AMELIA SATTERLY • DUNCAN SATTERLY • HARRY SATTERLY • PAUL SCARBOROUGH • JOHN SCLANDERS • MARK SCLANDERS • JULIAN SEEDS • DAVE SHEPPARD • JOSHUA SHEPPARD • ANDREW SHERWIN • COLIN SHERWIN • MICHAEL SIMPSON • DAVE SMALL •

# OUR FANS S-W

ALAN SMITH • ALYSANDRA SMITH • BEATRIX SMITH • CAITLIN SMITH • DAVID SMITH • HARRY SMITH • JENNY SMITH • JOSHUA SMITH • PETER SNELL • ANDY SNUGGS • JOE SNUGGS • ALISON SPARKE • MORGAN SPARKE • STEPHEN SPARKE • ANGELA ROSALIE SPENCER • BARRY SPENCER • BEN SPENCER • CHRISTOPHER PAUL SPENCER • CRAIG JORDAN SPENCER • DARREN SPENCER • HAZEL BROOKE SPENCER • JACK SPENCER • JASON SPENCER • LIBBY SPENCER • MARTIN SPENCER • PAUL SPENCER • PAUL SPENCER • TOBY CHRISTOPHER SPENCER • MARK SPIDY • ROB SPIERS • CHRIS STALLY • CHLOE STALLY-GIBSON • JOEL STALLY-GIBSON • BEN STEVENSON • DARYL STEVENSON • MIRANDA STEVENSON • TIM STEVENSON • JACK STOCK • JOE STOCK • PAUL STOCK • TOM STOCK • PAUL STRONG • TANK • JEFFREY TAVENDER • TRACEY TAVENDER • DALE THOMPSON • JACKIE THOMPSON • MARTYN DAVID THOMPSON • CORIN TIMS • GEORGE TIMS • IAN TIMS • ROISIN TIMS • JON TOMLIN • JONATHAN PETER TOMLIN • LORNA TOMLIN • LOTTIE TOMLIN • SALLY TOWNSEND • ADAM J TRANTER • HOWARD J TRANTER • HAYLEY TUCKER • NIGEL TUCKER • AVY TURNER • JACK WILLIAM TURNER • JAMES ANTONIO TURNER • MARK TURNER • TUBBY TYRRELL • ADAM ROY UPTON • ADRIAN VREEDE • CHARLIE WAINWRIGHT • GLADYS WAINWRIGHT • JEAN WAINWRIGHT • TED WAINWRIGHT • ALAN WALSTER • FRANCINE WALSTER • MARK WALSTER • PHIL WARREN • ELLIS AIDEN WATSON • HAYLEY WATSON • PETER WATSON • STUART WATSON • AIDAN WHITE • ALAN WHITE • ELLIOT WHITE • GRAEME WHITE • KEITH WHITE • MARK WHITE • PHILIP WHITE • PETER WHITEHEAD • CHLOE WHITESIDE • EDDA WHITESIDE • MARTIN WHITESIDE • THOMAS WHITESIDE • IAN WHYTE • ROB WILLARD • TIM WILLETT • ANDY WILLIAMS • DEREK WILLIAMS • GILLIAN WILLIAMS • DEBBIE & ROGER WINCHESTER • KIRBY THOMAS JAMES WING • MARTIN JAMES WING • RILEY THOMAS JAMES WING • TREVOR JAMES WING • JOHN WISE • CHRISTINE WOOD • CHRISTOPHER WOOD • MARK WOOD • TOBY WOOD • HAZEL WRAY • NICK WRIGHT • ADAM WYATT • FAYE WYATT • GARY WYATT • IAN WYATT • JAN WYATT • JULIA WYATT • MICHAEL WYATT

ENGLAND
RUGBY